Getting Started with Open Source Technologies

Applying Open Source Technologies with Projects and Real Use Cases

Sachin Rathee
Amol Chobe

Apress®

Getting Started with Open Source Technologies: Applying Open Source Technologies with Projects and Real Use Cases

Sachin Rathee
Florida, FL, USA

Amol Chobe
New Jersey, NJ, USA

ISBN-13 (pbk): 978-1-4842-8126-0
https://doi.org/10.1007/978-1-4842-8127-7

ISBN-13 (electronic): 978-1-4842-8127-7

Managing Director, Apress Media LLC: Welmoed Spahr
Acquisitions Editor: Divya Modi
Development Editor: James Markham
Coordinating Editor: Divya Modi
Copyeditor: Kim Burton Weisman

Cover designed by eStudioCalamar

Cover image designed by Freepik (www.freepik.com)

Distributed to the book trade worldwide by Springer Science+Business Media New York, 1 New York Plaza, Suite 4600, New York, NY 10004-1562, USA. Phone 1-800-SPRINGER, fax (201) 348-4505, e-mail orders-ny@springer-sbm.com, or visit www.springeronline.com. Apress Media, LLC is a California LLC and the sole member (owner) is Springer Science + Business Media Finance Inc (SSBM Finance Inc). SSBM Finance Inc is a **Delaware** corporation.

For information on translations, please e-mail booktranslations@springernature.com; for reprint, paperback, or audio rights, please e-mail bookpermissions@springernature.com.

Apress titles may be purchased in bulk for academic, corporate, or promotional use. eBook versions and licenses are also available for most titles. For more information, reference our Print and eBook Bulk Sales web page at http://www.apress.com/bulk-sales.

Any source code or other supplementary material referenced by the author in this book is available to readers on GitHub via the book's product page, located at www.apress.com/978-1-4842-8126-0. For more detailed information, please visit http://www.apress.com/source-code.

Printed on acid-free paper

My creative daughter, Smera, who makes me feel loved
My kind-hearted son, Niam, who inspires me to be generous
My beautiful wife, Nupur, who makes me
whole with her smiles
My commando dad, who makes me proud
with his achievements
My loving mom, who encourages me in everything I do
My amazing big brother, Nishant, who always cares for me
—Sachin

My mom, dad, and big bro
for helping me believe that anything is possible
My wife, Anagha,
and my children, Aditi and Atharva,
for their endless love and support
—Amol

Table of Contents

About the Authors

Sachin Rathee is a technologist and business executive with extensive experience in multiple facets of the software industry. Sachin has led many transformational projects using open source technologies for various enterprises. He is a strong proponent of open source and presented its value at multiple global conferences. Most recently, Sachin has led the realization of 5G and edge computing use cases in cloud-native environments. He has a bachelor's degree in engineering and a master's degree in business. Administration.

Amol Chobe is a solutions architect leader with more than 20 years of experience across numerous industries such as telecommunications and finance. He specializes in driving technology-based solutions into business-valued solutions based on customer needs and goals.

Amol has been a big advocate of the open source community and has given several presentations worldwide focusing on various open source projects. Lately, he has been working on cloud economics for hybrid and multi-clouds. He has a master's degree in computer engineering.

About the Technical Reviewer

 **Markus** is a Java Champion, former Java EE Expert Group member, founder of JavaLand, reputed speaker at Java conferences around the world, and a very well-known figure in the Enterprise Java world. With more than 16 years of professional experience in the industry, he designed and developed large Enterprise-grade applications for Fortune 500 companies. As an experienced team lead and architect, he helped implement some of the largest integration projects in automotive, finance, and insurance companies. You can connect to him on LinkedIn at www. linkedin.com/in/markuseisele/or follow him on Twitter at https:// twitter.com/myfear.

Introduction

Welcome to *Getting Started with Open Source Technologies: Applying Open Source Technologies with Projects and Real Use Cases.* If you are looking to understand what open source is, how open source operates, which industries are actively involved in open source, and open source security aspects, this is the right book for you.

Who Should Read This Book

This book is most suited for enterprises (developers/operators/ management) and students who want to get a 360-degree view of open source no matter how early or advanced they are in their adoption of any open source technology.

This book is based on real-world projects and use cases to help you understand the open source ecosystem better.

What Is Covered in the Book

This book has nine chapters. Each chapter progressively builds on the previous ones such that the readers get a good understanding of how various aspects of open source interrelate.

- Chapter 1 describes how the concept of open source started with the Free Software Foundation and Open Source Initiative. This chapter describes the open source community development process and discusses its current state.

- Chapter 2 delves into comparisons between the terms open source and open standards and how they interoperate. The chapter also discusses their interdependence with several examples.

- Chapter 3 goes into licensing terminology and explains the importance of various popular open source licenses. It also helps understand how to profit from open source and lists important open source projects for the licenses covered.

- Chapter 4 is about securing open systems. It covers security in the software development life cycle in the context of open source and how to handle vulnerability management. It also gives insights into policies and compliance and then goes over different security organizations.

- Chapter 5 explains infrastructure requirements for IT components, including computing, networks, and storage. It also lists various open source projects specific to these components.

- Chapter 6 covers basic concepts of emerging technologies like artificial intelligence, machine learning, and the Internet of Things and their use cases across industries. It explains these technologies using various open source projects and tools.

- Chapter 7 deals with the use of open source technologies in various industries. While doing so, it lists some of the most popular projects used today. Industries covered include aerospace, agriculture, automotive, energy, gaming, healthcare, manufacturing, telecom, and various cross-industry initiatives.

- Chapter 8 examines various trends in the open source world using information from GitHub. It gives a view of the most popular licenses, projects, programming languages, and contributors.

- Chapter 9 is the book's final chapter, which talks about the path forward for open source technologies. This chapter looks at what it takes to build a better and sustainable path for open source and discusses school curricula, tools, and industry programs. This chapter concludes by looking at current industry trends and upcoming innovations where open source technologies can help.

CHAPTER 1

Open Source: How We Got Here

In today's world, open source technology is considered the backbone of digital innovation and modernization. So, what does *open source* mean? It is loosely defined as software that anyone can modify and share as its design is easily accessible to the public.

Open source technologies help increase the pace of innovation by being open to collaboration, leading to the free exchange of innovative ideas within the communities. Suppose an end user or a developer finds a particular technology or a project fascinating. In that case, they can download the software and try it out. They can see what it does and if it serves their needs. If it does, they can choose to join the open source project and contribute to it. They can also use it as a base or foundation to create something new. Millions of people around the globe use open source technologies today.

One of the leading examples of open source technology is the Android operating system started by Google. Android is an open source operating system initially created for mobile devices. Other open source software examples include the Apache web server, the Mozilla Firefox browser, LibreOffice, and the Linux operating system.

This chapter defines the term *open source* and explains its advantages, challenges, and current state of affairs.

© Sachin Rathee and Amol Chobe 2022
S. Rathee and A. Chobe, *Getting Started with Open Source Technologies*,
https://doi.org/10.1007/978-1-4842-8127-7_1

Free Software Foundation

The free software and open source era began in the mid-1980s. In September 1983, Richard Stallman started the GNU project. GNU is an acronym for GNU's Not Unix! [1-1]. By design, GNU is like Unix but without Unix code and uses "free" software. The main objective of this project was to create a Unix-like operating system with openly available source code that could be copied, changed, and redistributed. Additional programs, applications, and libraries were released under the auspices of the GNU Project.

Note   Unix is a portable, multitasking, multiuser operating system developed in 1969 at the Bell Labs research center.

The Free Software Foundation (FSF) was established in 1985 as a non-profit organization promoting free software development. Under the leadership of Richard Stallman, this foundation continued supporting GNU projects [1-2]. From FSF's point of view, free software empowers the users to run, edit, share, and distribute the software. The emphasis was on free software as a matter of liberty, not price.

The FSF considers software "free" if it gives users the following four essential freedoms. These freedoms are the four crucial pillars of FSF.

- The freedom to execute the program as you desire and for any reason

- The freedom to analyze how the program operates and modify it

- The freedom to redistribute copies

- The freedom to circulate copies of your updated/ modified variants to others

Access to the source code is a prerequisite for the second and fourth pillars. The main objective of these freedoms is to allow the entire community to benefit from modifications made by anyone.

By the late 1980s and early 1990s, most developer communities used GNU. They collaborated on the code and fixed bugs that they would detect while using the software. FSF continues to educate the developers about free software through various resources, articles, and in-person advocacy.

The Linux Era

During the same time when FSF was formed, the hardware industry was undergoing evolution too. In 1985, the first x86 microprocessor with a 32-bit instruction set called 80386 was released by Intel. The 80386 significance was that it maintained backward compatibility with Intel's previous processors, which allowed it to run existing PC software. This backward compatibility was a significant milestone in the world of x86 hardware. This opened doors further for the creation of much more portable software which could run on multiple hardware architectures, and this helped to generate a knowledge pool of technical expertise due to easier access to the portable software and hardware in general

In 1991, in Helsinki, Finland, a computer science student at the University of Helsinki, Linus Torvalds, purchased a personal computer with an Intel 386 CPU. Torvalds started work on a new kernel and a free operating system. This project was developed using Minix. Torvalds used the GNU C compiler for the creation of this new kernel. This kernel was eventually named Linux. On August 25, 1991, Linus Torvalds announced the Linux system in a Usenet newsgroup forum.

> **Note**   Minix is a lightweight operating system inspired by Unix. Andrew Tannenbaum designed it for education purposes.
>
> Usenet is an Internet-based network of discussion groups. It is a forum where people share messages through Usenet servers.

The following is Linus Torvalds' announcement [1-3].

From: torvalds@klaava.Helsinki.FI (Linus Benedict Torvalds)
Newsgroups: comp.os.minix
Subject: What would you like to see most in minix?
Summary: small poll for my new operating system
Message-ID:
Date: 25 Aug 91 20:57:08 GMT
Organization: University of Helsinki

Hello everybody out there using minix -

I'm doing a (free) operating system (just a hobby, won't be big and professional like gnu) for 386(486) AT clones. This has been brewing since april, and is starting to get ready. I'd like any feedback on things people like/dislike in minix, as my OS resembles it somewhat (same physical layout of the file-system (due to practical reasons) among other things).

I've currently ported bash(1.08) and gcc(1.40), and things seem to work. This implies that I'll get something practical within a few months, and I'd like to know what features most people would want. Any suggestions are welcome, but I won't promise I'll implement them :-)

Linus (torvalds@kruuna.helsinki.fi)

PS. Yes - it's free of any minix code, and it has a multi-threaded fs.

It is NOT portable (uses 386 task switching etc), and it probably never will support anything other than AT-harddisks, as that's all I have :-(.

Linus Torvalds initially distributed the Linux kernel under a license that he created solely for this project [1-4]. Linux and GNU developers combined GNU components with the Linux kernel, making it a fully functional and free operating system. Due to objections raised against the original license rule that prohibited commercial distribution of the software, Linus Torvalds decided to distribute this operating system under GPL license, starting with the release of Linux 0.12.

The Cathedral and Bazaar Approaches

In 1997, at a Linux conference, an American software developer Eric Raymond presented two fundamental approaches to building software: Bazaar and Cathedral. He wrote an essay on this topic, and eventually, it became a full-length book.

Cathedral software is where a group of developers come together to code, find bugs, and fix those bugs. Then when the product is ready, they ship the product. This is similar to building a cathedral where everything is crafted and installed before allowing the public to see it. This approach, however, takes a lot of time.

On the other hand, the *Bazaar* software approach is free, running where there is no central control. Different developers, like vendors at a bazaar, offer different approaches to various problems, and these developers improve functionality or fix bugs as they see a need. Development is a collaborative process in this approach. This approach helps in releasing software early and often.

In this essay, Raymond compares the Linux approach (Bazaar) to the GNU approach (Cathedral) and finds the former more responsive to user needs. The essay received significant attention in the developer's community. It was one of the key factors that motivated Netscape Corporation to publish their crucial Netscape Communicator suite as free software. Netscape wanted to boost its business by tapping into a virtually unlimited developer talent pool for its next-generation browsers and thwarting competition from Microsoft's Internet Explorer. This source code consequently became the origin for Thunderbird and Mozilla Firefox.

The Open Source Initiative

The term *open source* was created in a session led by Eric Raymond after the notification of the release of the Netscape Communicator source code. This session was attended by industry stalwarts like Michael Tiemann, Sam Ockman, Jon Hall, Larry Augustin, and Todd Andersen on February 3, 1998, in Palo Alto, California.

The session attendees realized that the awareness around the Netscape decision had produced an opportunity to teach and promote the advantage of an open development process in the software and business development community. During the session, there was a common consensus that Netscape's announcement around releasing code has demonstrated a practical way to interlock with potential developers' expertise from the community.

To distinguish themselves, Eric Raymond and other session attendees started looking for a label or a term that would identify this initiative. They eventually agreed on the term *open source*, which was initially suggested by Christine Peterson [1-5]. The term gained much traction with early support from Linus Torvalds and founding members of Apache, Perl, Python, representatives from the Internet Engineering Task Force (IETF), and the Internet Software Consortium.

In late February 1998, Eric Raymond and Bruce Perens jointly founded the Open Source Initiative (OSI) as an educational, stewardship, and advocacy group. Raymond was the first president of OSI, and Perens was the first vice president. An initial Board of Directors included Russ Nelson, Brian Behlendorf, Ian Murdock, and Chip Salzenberg.

One of the main objectives of OSI is to engage and bring open source communities together effectively. Other objectives include collaboration, advocacy, and promotion of awareness regarding the importance of non-proprietary or open source software.

One of the key challenges for the OSI was to create proper criteria for considering a license to be open source. To handle this, OSI's first task was to draft the Open Source Definition (OSD) to determine whether the software license could be labeled open or not. Bruce Perens took input from the Debian developers and wrote OSD based on the Debian Free Software Guidelines. Next, OSI created an open source certification process that any license could use to verify its category.

Note   Debian is also known as Debian GNU/Linux. Ian Murdock established the Debian project on August 16, 1993. It is a GNU/Linux distribution consisting of free and open source software developed by the community-supported Debian Project.

For comparison purposes, *open source* is a development method for software that harnesses the power of the community and transparency of the process. In contrast, the OSI is a non-profit corporation formed to educate and advocate the benefits of open source.

The Open Source Definition

Open source is not limited to getting your hands around the software's source code. The distribution conditions of open source software must adhere to the following ten principles.

- **Free Redistribution**: No restrictions around selling or giving away

- **Source Code**: Must have access to actual source code

- **Derived Works**: Allow the modification and derived works

- **Integrity of the Author's Source Code**: May restrict distribution in modified form only in specific cases

- **No Discrimination Against Persons or Groups**: Do not lock out anyone out of the process, any person or a group is equally eligible to contribute to reap the maximum benefit of the process.

- **No Discrimination Against Fields of Endeavor**: Not limited to any specific domain

- **Distribution of License**: No additional license needed for derivatives

- **License Must Not Be Specific to a Product**: No dependency on the program's being limited to specific software distribution

- **License Must Not Restrict Other Software**: No restriction on other software

- **License Must Be Technology-Neutral**: Flexibility to choose any individual technology

The detailed descriptions of the criteria are documented on opensource.org [1-6]. OSI protects and promotes the open source definition to institute an open source ecosystem throughout the world.

FSF and OSI Comparisons

From the FSF point of view, software must always be free; the users have the freedom to copy, run, share, analyze, change, and enhance the software. Licenses authorized by the FSF do not allow the software code to be closed again. FSF requires its followers to use only free software and does not allow the provision of proprietary software.

Groups that support OSI are more pragmatic than ideological. They believe it is best to have source code to modify, but they do not mandate code availability. They don't require all the software in the world to be free.

Richard Stallman states the following in the article "Why Open Source Misses the Point of Free Software" [1-7]: "The two terms relate to nearly the same type of software, but they imply different values. Open source is a development practice; free software is a movement for freedom and justice." This is a great reference article that describes the difference between FSF and OSI from Richard Stallman's point of view.

Open Source and Closed Source

Table 1-1 compares the open source software with the closed source software. Here closed source software can also be read as proprietary software.

The table covers the different features of the software and provides open source and closed source mapping to it.

Table 1-1. *Open Source and Closed Source Comparisons*

	Open Source	Closed Source
Owner	Community	Company
Pricing	Free	Vendor pricing
Developers	Developers from various backgrounds and experiences collaborate	Company employed developers
Team	Decentralized across the globe, large	Limited to company developers, relatively small
Requirements	Prioritized by the need of the community/user base	Market or customer-driven/ commercial requirement
End-user support	Community, wiki, forums	Support team and via training services by the company
Redistribution	Depends on the open source software license	Depends on the license agreement and terms
Bugs/issues	Feed into open source community, collaborate to resolve	Customer support/ ticketing system
Tools	Use open source commonly available tools	Defined by companies' in-house policies
Monopoly	Low risk	Medium to high risk
Upgrade	Very frequently When new releases or features are tested, based on community involvement	Typically defined cycle and based on new features and serious bug issues

Given the comparisons in Table 1-1, there are plenty of reasons why people choose open source. The following are some of the most common.

- **Open collaboration**: The ability to find open source communities across the globe and get help from them. It helps provide different perspectives that trigger the innovation.

- **Transparency**: The ability to check updated source code anytime and track all the changes that happened.

- **Innovation**: Opportunity to develop the product with the best features and capabilities. Open source allows experimentation and provides the ability to pivot if needed.

- **Flexibility**: Open source provides flexibility at a faster pace compared to commercial products. You can easily change or update the codebase to address problems specific to the business needs.

- **Cost of ownership**: The most prominent benefit of open source software is that it's free to use. It provides the ability to harness the power of the community (via online forums or blogs) to get any help for running the software or fixing any bugs.

- **Reliability**: Because open source is freely available and the community is very active, peer developers actively check the code, which improves the code's reliability by ensuring that code is tested more often.

- **Start small**: There is the ability to start with community versions and migrate to commercial versions.

Other Varieties of Software

Two additional terms are worth mentioning: FOSS, which is *free and open source software*, and FLOSS, which is *free/libre open source software*.

In the *Merriam-Webster Collegiate Dictionary*, one definition of the word *free* is "not costing or charging anything," and another one is "enjoying personal freedom: not subject to the control or domination of another." Due to this ambiguity of the word in English (for free vs. freedom), libre was chosen. Libre comes from the Latin word *līber* and shares its root with liberty. It signifies "the state of being free," in the sense of "having full freedom" or "liberty." Therefore, FSF advocates the use of the FLOSS term. You learned earlier in this chapter that the term *free software* was created by Richard Stallman; the *free* is about freedom to modify the software (and not about price).

There are other common terms, such as *freeware* and *shareware*. Freeware and shareware have nothing to do with open source. Freeware is software that can be obtained free of cost. Any user can get access to it or download and use it. One of the key aspects is that the freeware software does not grant any freedom of modifying or distributing as available in open source software. Freeware is closed source. One of the most famous examples of freeware is Adobe Acrobat Reader, the software that allows you to view PDF files.

Shareware is software that is freely distributed to users on a trial basis. One of the primary objectives of the shareware is to allow users to use the product before purchasing it. Shareware distribution sometimes has a time limit or has limited features to try or have advertisements to generate revenue for the developers. The best example of shareware is an antivirus company that allows users to download and test their software on a trial basis.

The Open Source Software Community Development Process

An open source project starts with an idea or concept. Once you have decided on the realization of this idea into a software project, try to take advantage of an existing open source project and "fork" it, if needed, to start your own. To fork or not to fork depends on the project's initial developer or maintainer's judgment on the benefits and drawbacks. It may be beneficial to use existing work to save time, but it might also add extra complexity if it needs any customizations specific to your needs. To commence development, you also need additional tooling such as source code management systems to store the source code and its archives and version control mechanisms to track the software versions.

Note   The meaning of *fork* is "to divide into branches or go separate ways." In software development, a fork is introduced when developers take source code from one software repository to develop a new project.

Open source development is community-driven. Figure 1-1 depicts the software development process.

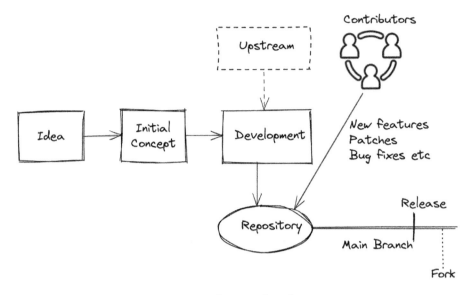

Figure 1-1. _The open source software development process_

Developers commit the source code (modifying the code and placing it back in the repositories) and create a distribution package (collection of software binaries that users can run) during the project's development process. As the interest in the project grows, many new contributors join the project and start contributing. They may join not just from the code development point of view but also for documentation or bug fixes.

Typically, contributors create a code branch and make changes or create patches for the code. It is the responsibility of the maintainers to judge which changes should be accepted. If the maintainer or project lead decides to incorporate the changes, these code changes become part of the main code branch. The community maintains the project even if a contributor stops being a part of the project. The community uses mailing lists and discussion boards for reporting bugs and providing feedback and fixes. All the community participants in an open source ecosystem have an opportunity to fix and improve the software.

The most significant advantage of an open source project is that several contributors are involved at a given time. They work together to fix defects or add new functionality, making it more robust. Because the source code is freely accessible, the open source community is very active and can offer help and perspectives beyond a single group's interest.

For an open source project, publishing the code is not enough. Open source projects are about fostering communities, sharing challenges, and taking responsibility for building better software. Project maintainers usually define or follow a code of conduct for the project. This code of conduct helps foster a harassment-free experience for everyone. A *code of conduct* is a document that determines rules of engagement for the project's participants. It empowers maintainers to facilitate constructive and healthy community behavior. For example, all the projects belonging to the Cloud Native Computing Foundation (CNCF) follow its code of conduct [1-8].

The Current State of Affairs

While vendor lock-in remains a big concern for proprietary software, more and more vendors are distributing the source code with their software to mitigate this concern. This is happening regardless of whether they plan to go fully open source or not. In parallel, major open source projects are capturing significant market shares, and they are turning out to be crucial for the growth of many industries.

In recent years, open source dynamics have transformed how projects are developed and delivered. Many big corporations have employee groups dedicated to making open source just as rich in functionality and features as enterprise software. Although the definition of *open source* might evolve further, community-based innovation continues technological advancement and help enterprises to innovate.

Based on the tremendous success of open source, a trend called InnerSource has emerged. It is where development teams adopt open source principles and best practices to work and collaborate more effectively. This trend is being adopted even for the development of proprietary software. It has led to collaboration between the various teams such that anyone from the organization can contribute to the code.

Note   *Vendor lock-in* makes a customer dependent on one vendor for products or a platform and hence unable to use another vendor without substantial investment in switching to a new platform.

Innovation and cultural shifts are playing a significant role in open source communities. Today's graduates, scientists, innovators, and engineers benefit from advancements in technology. This advancement has allowed the creation of global networks built by open source communities to share ideas freely. Communities are now free to create what they want to use, fostering a DIY (Do It Yourself) culture.

Conclusion

Open source software is a process or methodology that takes advantage of peer review among the development community and has the transparency in all its processes. It is revolutionary due to the involvement of communities of people.

Open source code has a life on its own. Even when its original authors have moved on, it is constantly updated through the support of its communities. Adherence to the project's standards and continued peer review ensures that open source code quality is maintained long-term.

When comparing open source software with free software, the former is considered a development practice, whereas the latter is a social movement. The FSF and the OSI played a significant role in evangelizing the idea of the community coming together and collaborating to create innovative open source projects.

References

[1-1] www.gnu.org

[1-2] www.fsf.org/news/fsf-and-gnu

[1-3] https://groups.google.com/g/comp.
os.minix/c/dlNtH7RRrGA/m/SwRavCzVE7gJ

[1-4] https://mirrors.edge.kernel.org/pub/
linux/kernel/Historic/old-versions/
RELNOTES-0.01

[1-5] https://opensource.org/history

[1-6] https://opensource.org/osd

[1-7] www.gnu.org/philosophy/open-source-
misses-the-point.html.en

[1-8] https://github.com/cncf/foundation/blob/
main/code-of-conduct.md

CHAPTER 2

Open Source and Open Standards

In the technology field, standards play a significant role in defining consistent behaviors between interacting systems. This chapter discusses what standards are, why they are needed, and how they apply to the open concept. Then, we dive deeper into industry-specific needs and look at several examples of standards specific to those industries. You also look at various open source examples that exist for these standards.

Open Standards

As discussed in the previous chapter, the concept of "open" applies to the ability to create, modify, view, or make use of something without any royalties or fees. We also discussed how the source code could be open or closed. Similarly, the standards can also be open or closed.

Let's make this more apparent with the help of an example. Consider a situation where you would like to send a document to your friends to read. You would want to make sure that your friends can view it on their devices such as laptops or smartphones. How to ensure that? The most straightforward way is to send it in a format that works on all devices. You have several options, including creating a Microsoft Word document file with a .doc extension, which allows you to view the file on

S. Rathee and A. Chobe, *Getting Started with Open Source Technologies*,
https://doi.org/10.1007/978-1-4842-8127-7_2

any Windows operating system (OS) device since it's a standard within Microsoft products. However, since it's not a standard for non-Microsoft-based devices (such as those running Linux OS), any default document applications on these non-Microsoft OS devices cannot load that file properly, if at all. This makes the .doc word file format a standard but limited to Microsoft only.

Now let's look at two different options: Adobe Acrobat PDF (.pdf) and Microsoft Word (.docx) formats. The PDF files are viewable on almost all devices, given that it's an open standard that's freely available for anyone to implement. Similarly, the .docx format, based on the open standard called Office Open XML, is viewable on virtually all types of devices with different operating systems. Therefore picking one of these two should be your choice when sending a document for all your friends to view easily.

Building Standards

Creating a standard requires a lot of knowledge specific to the domain for which standards are being developed. For example, organizations developing Wi-Fi standards need to understand wireless technology, regulations, and implementation challenges. Similarly, organizations developing standards for the travel industry need to know how various booking systems work.

Standards development organizations (SDOs) create and maintain industry standards. An SDO's charter is to develop, revise, promote, and help interpret various standards. Multiple SDOs often work on the same domain but with competing technologies leading to competing standards. This can be avoided via collaboration. Various SDOs may decide to collaborate on standards under a shared vision and distribute work based on factors like geography, experience, and current competence within their teams. Such a collaboration would reduce competition and increase the adoption of technologies.

SDO consists of several entities to help with various aspects of the standard development processes. These primarily consist of the following.

- **Staff**: These individuals get involved in the day-to-day functioning of the SDO. They help with scheduling, finances, organizing events, coordinating within various groups, and so on.

- **Board members**: This comprises executive-level leaders who are experienced in managing complex organizations. They help define policies governing the SDOs.

- **Contributors**: These are the volunteers who participate in the creation of standards. Enterprises may have employees who officially dedicate their time to this effort. However, it requires volunteering outside the usual working hours in most instances. The contributors may be classified depending on their expertise and involvement in specific areas or projects.

Developing a standard typically requires several steps, from introducing an idea to the final output. Figure 2-1 provides a generic view of the process.

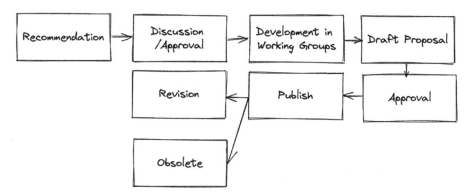

Figure 2-1. *Standards development process*

Although SDOs sometimes require a paid membership to participate and benefit as this helps with their costs, they should abide by at least the following tenets for an SDO to develop a truly open standard.

- **Publicly available**: The standards should be available to members and non-members alike.

- **Community-driven**: Although SDO members need to be capable and have the expertise necessary to create standards, members should not be restricted to one group or company. Joining SDO as a member should have minimum barriers to entry.

Open Source with Open Standards

Open source and open standards have a unique relationship. Technologies that have open standards can be implemented with closed source/proprietary products and still serve the purpose of interoperability. On the other hand, technologies that are not standardized or open yet may proliferate via broader acceptance of the open source implementations of these technologies, making these open implementations a standard themselves. Let's look at examples for both cases.

All televisions understand how to decode the air signals transmitted by TV stations. This is so because TV stations follow broadcasting standards that any TV manufacturer can implement. The implementation may be different, but the result is the same: you can watch your favorite channels on any TV set containing open or closed technology.

Now, let's look at a case where an open standard does not exist, and an open source project can lead to standardization. Today several browsers allow you to surf the internet. However, the choice of browsers may be limited to the operating system or hardware you use. The operating system's functionality is to provide standard services such as file, memory, and process management to the applications running on it. The implementation of operating systems might be different; however, the functionality provided to the applications remains the same. The same application, such as your Firefox browser, can run on these different operating systems as long as it's built for each OS separately. This is why you would see separate downloadable files for Firefox for different operating systems. Firefox, an open source software, abstracts all the different interfaces and allows you to get the same experience, something that cannot be done with a closed source software that was most likely built for a single OS owned by the browser's parent company. Furthermore, the open source community ensures that the software gets maximum compatibility with multiple operating systems. As the adoption of Firefox has increased, it has started to become a standard browser for various operating systems and devices.

Note   Given the success of open source browsers like Firefox, the latest browsers such as Edge from Microsoft and Chrome from Google are based on Chromium, another open source browser.

Let's look at another slightly different example: a new open source entrant surpassed a technology with closed source software. Apple owned the majority market share for iOS devices as it had a first-mover advantage. Today, however, Android-based devices own most of the market, and Android OS is used by multiple phone manufacturers who are eating into the iOS devices market. This shows how standardization tends to favor open alternatives. This is a case where a proprietary product may exist, but open source affects its market via wider adoption and thus standardization.

Standards in Practice

Standards are developed for different industries and geographies based on their specific requirements. International standards help with interoperability between various regions such as countries and continents, whereas national and regional standards cater to unique rules and regulations within countries/continents. Classification of these standards based on industries helps analyze the unique challenges they solve within these domains. While it is impossible to detail every technical standard development organization, we investigate some major SDOs from the communications, automotive and financial industries. We list any notable standards developed within them. We also list any relevant open source projects that provide implementations for those industries.

Standards in Communications Industry

The communications industry is one of the most standards-centric industries. Let's understand why that is the case with a simple example. Say you are trying to make a phone call to your friend. You are a Verizon customer while your friend is with AT&T. As you can imagine, for the call to be successful, both Verizon and AT&T need to have common standards to handle this communication. To complicate matters further, think about international calls wherein your friend is vacationing in another country. In this scenario, the call requires communication with an international carrier located in the same country as your friend. Since many US carriers are not global carriers, they have agreements with other carriers to provide service in locations outside of the United States. For these agreements to work, a separate standard between the national carriers of different countries is needed. Let's look at some of the standard organizations in the telecommunications industry which are helping to make these types of regional, national, or international communications happen.

International Telecommunication Union (ITU)

The International Telecommunication Union, founded in 1865, is one of the oldest international organizations [2-1]. It is a United Nations agency for information and communication technologies (ICTs).

ITU is broadly divided into the following three sectors.

ITU Radiocommunication Sector

Facilitates the global use of the radio spectrum and allocation of satellite orbits. It develops the standards for radiocommunication systems. It has about 1500 standards, all available online for free.

ITU Telecommunication Standardization Sector

Develops international standards called recommendations. These recommendations specify how telecommunication networks operate and interwork. There are about 4,000 recommendations in force today. Once the final, edited version is published, recommendations are available in electronic form, free of charge.

ITU Development Sector

It strives to provide affordable access to telecommunications to stimulate broader social and economic development. It impacts various facets of ICT adoption by developing policy and regulation frameworks, among other programs that could be adopted by multiple nations quickly.

ETSI

European Telecommunications Standard Institute is a European Standards Organization (ESO). It is a regional standards body creating standards for telecommunications, broadcasting, and communications networks and services. ETSI was founded to serve European needs; however, given its global perspective, many of its standards are now used all over the world. ETSI partners with other communications standards bodies to develop consistent standards.

ETSI has published over 40,000 standards and provides them free of charge. The standards are available in multiple formats from its website [2-2].

ETSI was responsible for delivering the Global System for Mobile Standard (better known as GSM), which helped define the 2G or second generation of cellular networks.

3GPP

The 3rd Generation Partnership Project (3GPP) [2-3] is a unique initiative that unites seven different standards organizations. ETSI is one of the seven SDOs. This setup helps facilitate cooperation between the partner organizations to produce the reports and specifications that define technologies in mobile/cellular specific technical areas.

As the name suggests, the initial charter of 3GPP was to produce technical specifications and technical reports for a 3G Mobile System. However, the scope was subsequently amended. The specifications now cover various mobile network generations, including fifth generation/5G cellular network technologies. 3GPP specifications are available free of charge.

A recent example of the 3GPP standard would be the architecture for the fifth generation/5G system for telecommunications. This specification is defined under TS 23.501.

CableLabs

Founded in 1988, CableLabs [2-4] is the research and development organization for the cable industry. It focuses on network technologies that help deliver broadband faster and better while providing the latest experiences in entertainment for connected devices.

Currently, CableLabs has more than 60 cable companies from all over the globe as its members. These member companies determine service requirements for the latest technologies and services. These requirements help develop new specifications, which drive participants' engineering decisions. All specifications are publicly available.

Well-known specifications developed by CableLabs include DOCSIS, which allows transmission of high-speed data to an existing cable television system.

CableLabs hosts several open source projects for the acceleration of industry acceptance. These include Chirpstack, Adrenaline project, and SNAPS, to name a few.

IETF

The Internet Engineering Task Force (IETF) [2-5] is a standards organization that deals with internet-specific architectures and technologies. Its mission is "To make the Internet work better by producing high quality, relevant technical documents that influence the way people design, use, and manage the Internet."

IETF achieves its mission using an open process where interested parties can participate and make their voices heard on the issues that need to be addressed. Core participants are volunteers who care about making the internet better. IETF is open to any interested individual, and standards created are available free of charge.

A well-known example of the IETF standard is the Transmission Control Protocol (TCP). It is defined under IETF RFC 793. This protocol forms the basis of reliable communications between packet-switched computer communication networks.

Open Source Implementations

Communications technology has many implementations in open source communities. Linux Foundation provides several components and platforms for these implementations. The following are some examples.

- **Open Network Automation Platform** is an orchestrator for deploying and managing network applications [2-6].

- **OpenDaylight** is a software-defined networking layer for managing networks [2-7].

- **OpenvSwitch** is a virtual switch [2-8].

- **OpenStack** is a virtual infrastructure manager for network applications [2-9].

Standards in Automotive Industry

Today's automotive industry is not the same as a few years back. Vehicles are getting smarter with advances in technology. They are no longer mere mechanical equipment but smart devices with many complex systems running in tandem. Nowadays, vehicles contain advanced programmable electronic circuitry and millions of lines of code to go with it. This gives vehicles the ability to control the engine, infotainment, communications, and driving or self-driving features. Therefore, standards governing the automotive industry have also advanced from only quality and safety to technology-specific needs in navigation, communication, and so on.

5GAA

The 5G Automotive Association [2-10] was formed in 2016 to collaborate between automotive, technology, and telecommunication companies to develop end-to-end mobility and transportation services solutions.

Its eight founding members were Daimler AG, Huawei, Intel, Ericsson, Nokia, BMW Group, AUDI AG, and Qualcomm. Membership has now grown to more than 130 companies.

5GAA consists of seven working groups that handle various facets of technology and business.

- Use cases and technical requirements

- System architecture and solution development

- Evaluation, testbeds, and pilots

- Standards and spectrum

- Business models and go-to-market strategies

- Regulatory and public affairs

- Security and privacy

5GAA provides inputs, recommendations, and contributions to other SDOs, such as 3GPP and ETSI, as part of its standard specification efforts. An example of this is 3GPP Technical Specification 22.186, which discusses service requirements for enhanced V2X scenarios.

AUTOSAR

AUTomotive **O**pen **S**ystem **AR**chitecture [2-11] is a global partnership that dates back to late 2002. It consists of vehicle manufacturers, service providers, suppliers, and companies from the automotive electronics, semiconductor, and software industry who pursue the following major goals.

- Meet vehicle requirements on availability and safety, software upgrades/ updates, and maintainability while increasing software reuse

- Improve scalability and flexibility of the systems

- Adopt COTS software and hardware to optimize costs

AUTOSAR has five main areas of standardization.

29

- **Classic platform** is focused on embedded systems with hard real-time and safety constraints.

- **Adaptive platform** is primarily for high-performance computing use cases such as autonomous driving.

- **Foundation** includes common parts of the classic and adaptive platforms, such as common communication bus protocols.

- **Acceptance tests** are system tests that validate the behavior of an AUTOSAR technology stack regarding the application software components and the communication bus.

- **Application interfaces** include the development of interface specifications that applications use in the stack. This allows software reuse and information exchange.

CCC

The Car Connectivity Consortium (CCC) [2-12] is a cross-industry organization involved in standardizing interfaces between vehicles and smartphones. The CCC member companies consist of smartphone and vehicle manufacturers and have more than 100 members today. CCC aims to increase interoperability between mobile devices and vehicles. CCC facilitates the coordination of mobile device OEMs and vehicle OEMs to build products with ease of use, convenience, security, privacy protections, and extensive capability. The CCC evaluates and certifies devices, cars, and apps for compliance and interoperability through well-defined certification processes.

Note   OEM stands for *original equipment manufacturer.* It is a company that makes devices from parts bought from other companies.

The following are the CCC's three main projects.

- **Digital Key** is involved in the standardization of technology for consumers to easily and securely use their mobile devices to access vehicles. It enables mobile devices to authenticate, store, and share digital keys.

- **MirrorLink** is involved in standardizing device control from within vehicles via the dashboard or steering wheel. It allows users to access certified applications on smartphones within their vehicles.

- **Car Data** is involved in developing a car data exchange to monetize car data. It acts as a central brokerage to connect suppliers of car data to those interested in utilizing that information to provide services.

Open Source Implementations

COMASSO project, a user group on AUTOSAR, provides open source implementation of the AUTOSAR platform.

Automotive Grade Linux (AGL) is another open source project building a Linux-based, open software platform for automotive applications.

Standards in Financial Industry

The world relies on transparent and well-documented financial transactions to run its economies smoothly. This requirement makes the financial industry one of the most regulated industries in the world. To keep economic disruptions to a minimum, changes in the financial sector are heavily scrutinized. The financial industry has invested heavily in information technology, and banks are becoming quite sophisticated in their use of IT.

ASC X9

The Accredited Standards Committee X9 (ASC X9) [2-13] is accredited by ANSI to develop the US financial services industry standards. X9 has alliances with multiple organizations involved in financial services and maintains US and international standards. These standards help improve payments and securities transactions while protecting data and facilitating the exchange of information.

Note   ANSI stands for American National Standards Institute. It is a non-profit organization that oversees the development of various standards in the United States.

The development process is open to any party interested in a standard under development. All development activities are fair, public, and documented for all members to see.

The following are some popular areas and technologies that X9 has standards in or is investigating.

- **Distributed ledger/blockchain** includes understanding the use of a transparent and decentralized technology to record financial transactions in a distributed ledger.

- **Quantum computing** includes understanding the risk to financial data secured via traditional computing with the advent of quantum computing.

- **Mobile payments** include developing a framework for mobile payments, such as payments to a person and businesses.

- **Cryptography** deals with enhanced communication security techniques via symmetric and asymmetric key cryptography.

X9 currently includes more than 100 member companies with 250 member representatives that help develop and maintain standards. There are about 125 American national and 27 international ISO standards during its 40 years of developing standards.

Open Source Implementations

The Fintech Open Source Foundation (FINOS), part of the Linux Foundation, helps drive open source communities within the financial industry. It supports several active open source projects.

Hyperledger is another open source community. It focuses on developing frameworks (e.g., Hyperledger Fabric, Sawtooth, Indy), tools (e.g., Hyperledger Caliper), and libraries (e.g., Hyperledger Ursa) for enterprise-grade blockchain deployments.

Conclusion

Although open standards and open source technologies differ, they have a synergistic relationship. Open standards provide uniformity in technology, whereas open source supports standardization with its implementation.

In cases where implementation of innovative solutions precedes standardization, the open source implementations themselves influence or become the standards. This could be the case even when proprietary products exist already.

A lot of industries are standardizing their technologies via several standard development organizations. These organizations foster better relationships between their member companies in areas of common technological interest.

From a standards development organization's point of view, it is in the best interest of an SDO itself to be open. Openness allows for several benefits, such as the following.

- Wider acceptance due to the availability of standards for anyone to implement

- Lower competition with other SDOs working on similar technology

- Increased Innovation with increased participation from various enterprises and individuals

- Better collaboration with multiple enterprises participating together in various working groups

One understated benefit of standardization that we often overlook is waste reduction. In 2021, the European Commission asked all phone manufacturers to standardize USB-C chargers. This has the benefit of reuse, as the same chargers could now be used with any phone. Similar benefits can be achieved in other areas of technology via standardization.

References

[2-1] www.itu.int/en/Pages/default.aspx

[2-2] www.etsi.orgstandards/get-standards#Pre-defined%20Collections

[2-3] www.3gpp.org

[2-4] www.cablelabs.com

[2-5] www.ietf.org

[2-6] www.onap.org

[2-7] www.opendaylight.org

[2-8] www.openvswitch.org

[2-9] www.openstack.org

[2-10] https://5gaa.org

[2-11] www.autosar.org

[2-12] https://carconnectivity.org

[2-13] https://x9.org

CHAPTER 3

Open Source Licenses

A software license permits the user to use its software in a particular manner. The license could be proprietary or open source. The former is much more restrictive than the latter on how a user may use it.

This chapter explains the various aspects of open source license creation and looks at current open source software licenses. You also learn how to pick a suitable license as a creator of open source software.

For enterprises, commercialization is an important aspect. Therefore, you look at how enterprises should pick the right open source software based on its license to help meet its commercialization goals.

Trusted Open Source Licenses

Today there are numerous open source licenses as well as free software licenses. It is a humongous task to keep up with them, let alone decide which one to use. Understanding license implications for a project can make adopting open source or free software much more complicated and confusing.

The Open Source Initiative (OSI) [3-1] was formed to alleviate these issues and help promote open source software. OSI maintains an Open Source Definition (OSD) which lists the criteria for open source licenses.

© Sachin Rathee and Amol Chobe 2022
S. Rathee and A. Chobe, *Getting Started with Open Source Technologies*,
https://doi.org/10.1007/978-1-4842-8127-7_3

For a license to be approved by the OSI, it must undergo its license review process. The review process ensures that licenses conform to existing community norms and expectations. A license can be approved as an open source license if it complies with these criteria. This includes allowing the software to be freely used, modified, and shared.

Similarly, the Free Software Foundation maintains a list of licenses that it considers adhering to its philosophy. It provides a comprehensive list of free licenses and their compatibility with other licenses.

Additionally, the Software Package Data Exchange (SPDX), an open standard for communicating software bills of material information (including licenses), provides a license list. The list consists of various licenses and exceptions used in software, hardware, data, and documentation.

Licensing Options

Open source licenses can broadly be categorized as follows.

- **Permissive** licenses guarantee the freedom to use, modify and redistribute the software. They do not even require that the modified versions remain free and publicly available and generally require only that the original copyright notice be retained. The license allows easy creation of proprietary derivatives from actual work.

- **Reciprocal** licenses provide the user with the freedom to use the software. However, it requires that the same rights (as the original software) are preserved in all the derivatives. This is achieved by requiring that the modified source code be made available to users for further software modifications. *Copyleft* software licenses come under this category; it is a play on the word *copyright*. Copyright provides its owner exclusive and legal rights for a piece of work.

According to the GNU, "Proprietary software developers use copyright to take away the users' freedom; we use copyright to guarantee their freedom. That's why we reverse the name, changing *copyright* into *copyleft*." A copyleft license could itself be considered weak or strong. A strong copyleft license covers the original software and any code that links to it. Therefore, using the strong copyleft makes the complete software product strong copylefted. A weak copyleft license covers the original software only, allowing even proprietary code to link to functions of the original software without violating its license terms.

In comparing the two options, enterprises consider permissive licenses more favorable. Permissive licenses give enterprises the ability to create a competitive edge over an existing open source project without a need to share it with anyone.

Another critical aspect is that many software products could integrate other software components with different categories of licenses. In such a scenario, enterprises should understand the compatibility aspect of such licenses. From the definitions, you can see how combining a component with a reciprocal license with a permissive one is easier as long as the final product falls under a more restrictive reciprocal license. Having the final product under permissive licensing may not always be possible, depending on restrictions on reciprocal licenses of the components used.

Choosing the Appropriate License for Your Work

As a software creator, you can assign any license you please. You have the liberty to select even a proprietary license. Proprietary licenses may be an option if you are part of an enterprise that has enough resources to build, improve and maintain the software in the future. However, users who buy proprietary software should remember that the software lives as long as its creators remain in business. If they go out of business, then there is a good possibility that the software will soon be worthless due to no further updates, upgrades, or bug fixes.

On the other hand, the open source paradigm assures that software is always available for anyone to use, even if creators are no longer involved. Open source projects can also grow extensively with the help of considerable community resources. These resources can improve the project continuously without the creators' involvement.

Picking the correct open source license could be done based on the end goal. If you want your project to attract large enterprises, then permissive licenses are the best choice. Alternatively, you may want your project to appeal to true open source proponents who do not wish their code and contributions used in proprietary software. In that case, reciprocal licenses are good candidates. Of course, if you're making contributions to an existing project, it can get complicated. In that scenario, you are most likely bound by the initial license clauses, which could make you release your modified project under the same license as the original work.

Every licensor has to decide whether their work is so unique that it warrants the creation of a new license for their open source project. Generally, the answer would most likely be *no.* You could base it on two primary reasons. First, there are already so many licenses approved by OSI that the chances of one not meeting your requirements are slim. Second, if you care about open source, it would be better to pick the most prevalent open source license available and increase the chance of adoption of your project immensely.

Next, let's look at some of the popular open source licenses approved by OSI.

The Apache License

The Apache License is a permissive license released via the Apache Software Foundation (ASF) [3-2]. ASF uses this license to release projects maintained under it. However, the license is not restricted to software products under ASF only and can be used by non-foundation projects. It permits users to release the modified parts of the code under any license. However, all the unmodified areas of the software remain under the same license (the Apache License).

The Apache License has gone through a few iterations. The original license (Apache License 1.0) is used with older software packages. In 2000 ASF approved the Apache License version 1.1. The new version removed one of the clauses, better known as the advertising clause. Removal of the clause meant that the derived software products were not required to include ASF attribution in their advertising materials. Instead, it is only needed in the derived product documentation. Removing this clause reduces the burden on enterprises because advertising for all open source components and the derived work under similar licensing requirements, which make a final product, might not be feasible.

In 2004, ASF approved Apache License 2.0, the most current license version. This version has changed in the language and definitions compared to previous versions. The most crucial change worth highlighting is the grant of patent licenses. This clause assures that patents are not asserted against users of the software product, who have the rights to use it under the version 2.0 license. Furthermore, the clause disallows contributors from pursuing patent royalties from any software users, including their contribution to the project.

Apache License 2.0 is great for companies of various sizes. Startups, which generally have limited funding, can use the software without worrying about expensive legal issues regarding patents. On the other hand, it also allows any enterprise to keep their competitive edge intact by not releasing their code modifications if they so desire.

Prominent Projects That Use this License

Kubernetes [3-3] is one of the most well-known examples. It is the container orchestration platform for automating containerized applications' deployment, scaling, and management.

The Android Open Source Project (AOSP) [3-4] is another project under Apache License 2.0. It is an open source operating system for mobile devices widely used by many phone manufacturers. Apache License 2.0 is the preferred license for all parts of the AOSP project.

One of the most well-known web servers, Apache HTTP Server [3-5], is also licensed under Apache 2.0.

The Berkeley Software Distribution License (BSD License)

Berkeley Source Distribution (BSD) licenses refer to a class of licenses under the permissive licensing category. Although there are multiple variants, the 1990 BSD license with four clauses is commonly considered the original BSD license. This license required users to include the copyright notice, list of conditions, and disclaimers with redistributions. It also required prior consent from the contributors and copyright holders to use their names to promote or endorse the derived products. Additionally, it had an advertising clause that required the mention of the copyright holder in advertising material.

Like the Apache License, the BSD license dropped advertisement requirements in its next iteration. This new version became the 3-clause BSD license [3-6].

Another simplified license came into existence with only two clauses. This license, aptly referred to as the 2-clause BSD license [3-7], only requires users to include the copyright notice, list of conditions, and disclaimers with redistributions. It omits the clause regarding consent for endorsement.

Prominent Projects That Use this License

The Go programming language [3-8], popular with cloud-based applications, AI, and data science, is licensed under BSD.

The widely used Nginx web server [3-9] is licensed under the BSD license.

The FreeBSD operating system [3-10] is licensed under the BSD license. Bionic software [3-11], a standard C library implementation for the Android operating system, is also under the BSD license.

The GNU General Public License

The GNU General Public License [3-12], or simply GPL, refers to a series of licenses created by Richard Stallman. The GPL license falls in the reciprocal category of the licenses. The first version released addressed the issue of compatibility with other licenses. Section 2B of the license states that if a part of the software uses GPL, the final product should be licensed under it. The language used here ensures that GPL software components used with restrictive licenses are not allowed, thus maintaining the principles of free software.

However, the first version did not address the patent infringement litigation issue. Therefore, the second version of GPL addressed this in section 7 of the license terms: if any additional conditions are imposed on the product due to patent infringement, those conditions should not contradict the license. It provides the following example.

If a patent license would not permit royalty-free redistribution of the Program by all those who receive copies directly or indirectly through you, then the only way you could satisfy both it and this License would be to refrain entirely from distribution of the Program.

While GPLv2 was being developed, a realization regarding software libraries crept in. Consider the C library, which provides macros, type definitions, and various functions and operating system services. Given its need, even the proprietary systems or compilers come with a C library. Therefore, making the C library available only to free software would discourage the use of the C library. Given this predicament, a strategic decision was made to introduce a different license for libraries called Library General Public License, or LGPL. This license was complementary with GPLv2 and started with the same version, version 2. The license was later renamed to GNU Lesser General Public License in version 2.1 (LGPLv2.1). The LGPL is categorized as weak copyleft while GPL falls under strong copyleft licenses.

The LGPL requires that the larger program using the LGPL library is considered a derivative of the LGPL'd library. The developer can distribute the resulting larger executable program under the terms of his or her own choice. Still, those terms must allow users to modify the executable program and reverse engineering for debugging those modifications.

Additionally, if the LGPL'd library is statically linked with the other software, the developer must also provide the linkable object code version (or the source code of the other software). These are demanding requirements. The GPL with a classpath exception provides a better alternative in certain cases. Like the LGPL, the GPL with a classpath exception allows a developer to link the classpath library with different programs, creating a larger program. This resulting program can be distributed under the terms of the developer's choice. But it differs from LGPL. The GPL with a classpath exception doesn't allow modifications to the larger program or reverse engineering. Also, it doesn't mandate access to the object code version of the program.

Later, GPL version 3 was introduced to provide further improvements. Most notably, GPL version 3 added definitions for the key terms used in the license. Additionally, it handled digital restrictions management issues where hardware used to run a GPL licensed application may not allow the modified code to run on it. GPLv3 also provides explicit patent protection. With the previous version, users relied on an implicit patent license to prevent litigations for patent infringement. GPLv3 provides users with explicit patent protection from the program's contributors and redistributors. The other significant change was to make the GPL compatible with some additional free software licenses that were initially incompatible with GPL v2.

There was still one unique case that GPL licenses did not cover. There was no clause in GPL that covered the use case where the software was accessed over the network rather than distributed. This is true in a *software as a service* (SaaS) model. Hence a SaaS provider did not have to make the source code available. To handle this loophole, a new license was created by Affero, Inc. in March 2002. This was called the Affero General Public License (AGPLv1) and was based on GPLv2. The Free Software Foundation published a new license similar to AGPL, based on GPLv3, and called it GNU AGPLv3.

Prominent Projects That Use this License

Linux kernel, which is in use by many operating systems, including the GNU operating system, is licensed under GPL. MySQL [3-13] database's community version and MariaDB [3-14], a fork of MySQL, are provided under the GPL license.

The Drupal open source content management system [3-15] is licensed under GPLv2 or later. Git software [3-16], which is used to track changes in files, uses GPL and LGPL licenses.

edX platform [3-17], which provides online courses, is licensed under AGPL.

The MIT License

The MIT License [3-18] is a permissive license created by the Massachusetts Institute of Technology. It is one of the shortest licenses giving a lot of flexibility in its use and making it compatible with many copyleft licenses. The conciseness has most likely resulted in the highest use of this license compared to any other open source license on GitHub.com, according to a 2015 blog post [3-19].

According to the license, you can copy, use, modify, merge, publish, distribute, sublicense, and sell copies of the software. You have no restrictions on its distribution. The only limitation is that the software should include the copyright and permission notice.

Prominent Projects That Use this License

Microsoft's .NET platform [3-20] was released under the MIT License. The Godot game engine [3-21] was also released under the MIT License; its source code is available on GitHub.

Keras [3-22], an interface for the TensorFlow [3-23] library, is under the MIT License. TensorFlow is used for machine learning and artificial intelligence. Other examples are Lua programming language [3-24] employed for embedded use, PuTTY [3-25], a free implementation of SSH and Telnet for Windows and Unix platforms, and PowerShell hosted on GitHub.

The Mozilla Public License

The Mozilla project was created in 1998 with the Netscape browser suite source code [3-26]. While doing so, Netscape created the Netscape Public License (NPL). This new license was unique compared to other open source licenses as it allowed relicensing of open code as proprietary [3-27]. This relicensing option did not bode well with the open source community. There was an alternative in plain sight for the community to use, however. It was the Mozilla Public License (MPL), which was created at the same time as NPL but without the relicensing capability. MPL was initially used for only the new code written to interact with NPL-covered code but seemed appropriate for general use.

Pretty soon, MPL went through a minor update. The new version, MPL-1.1, had a few essential updates. It clarified patenting terms such as "patent claims." It also added a section to handle multiple-licensed code where the initial developer could further utilize the code under MPL or other alternative licenses. This allowed developers to pick their preferred licenses to work with MPL.

Early MPL versions were found to be incompatible with GPL. Hence their use was discouraged by the Free Software Foundation. To address this challenge, MPL version 2.0 was released. This version addressed compatibility with GPL and other licenses like Apache, making it a better reciprocal license. The OSI also approved this new version.

Prominent Projects That Use This License

Mozilla foundation has its projects under MPL. Well-known examples include Firefox [3-28], a famous web browser. Another example is Bugzilla [3-29], the general-purpose bug tracking system.

Many other projects utilizing MPL do not fall under the Mozilla Foundation. These include LibreOffice [3-30], the freely available office suite, and RabbitMQ, one of the most widely deployed message brokers [3-31].

The Eclipse Public License

The Eclipse Public License (EPL) is a reciprocal license that falls into the weak copyleft category. The EPL-licensed software users can use, modify, copy, and distribute the work and its modified versions.

The latest version of EPL is version 2.0, finalized in 2017. As stated by the Eclipse Foundation, updating to version 2.0 was to bring it in line with changes in the industry [3-32]. Most notable changes include making the license suitable for scripting languages such as JavaScript and including an option to add a secondary license for GPL-2.0+ compatibility.

The latter change is quite significant as several Eclipse projects require GPL compatibility. The prior solution was to dual-license projects under the EPL-1.0 and the BSD. This approach, however, eliminated the copyleft provisions and led to incompatibility with GPL.

Note   *Dual licensing* means distributing the same software under two (or more) different sets of terms. Dual-licensed software allows recipients to choose the terms they want to obtain the software. Dual licensing is generally done to accomplish different business models and license compatibility. As an example, the MySQL database management system uses a dual licensing model. MySQL can be under a proprietary license for licensees who want to create and commercially distribute proprietary derivative works incorporating MySQL. On the other hand, MySQL can be under the GPL for licensees who want to incorporate MySQL into a product later distributed likewise under the GPL.

Prominent Projects That Use this License

The Eclipse Foundation uses the EPL. Their most notable project is the Eclipse integrated development environment (IDE) [3-33]. Eclipse Che [3-34] is also under the same license.

JUnit [3-35], the unit testing framework for the Java programming language, is licensed under EPL. Jetty, the Java web server and Java Servlet container, uses EPL too.

License Proliferation

When open source was introduced, only a handful of open source licenses were available. To encourage better adoption of open source, OSI encouraged the enterprises or individuals working on various projects to use the open source licenses already available or create ones better suited to their needs.

This led to a significant increase in licenses because many users wanted to create something unique to their situation. The OSI approved many of these new licenses that followed the OSD. Even though all these licenses promoted reading, modifying, and sharing source code, they were often incompatible with existing licenses. Since it is impossible to know which new licenses would be adopted more than the others, the proliferation of licenses continued unrestricted. The users could decide what they wanted to use.

OSI set up a committee to better understand the issues around current licenses and make recommendations. As part of its work, the committee created and submitted a report of its findings. This report is now available on the OSI website [3-36]. It highlighted the following aspects.

- **Understanding license proliferation**: This primarily considered three main aspects.

    - Too many choices to choose from

- License incompatibility

- Difficulty in tracking compliance in a multilicense scenario

- **OSI's role in dealing with license proliferation**: Besides checking for compliance with OSD, OSI provided the following guidelines for licenses.

  - The license must not be duplicative.

  - The license must be written simply and understandable.

  - The license must be reusable.

It further suggested providing the capability to search existing licenses based on the needs of the licensors.

- **Creation of license categories**: The following categories superseded the recommended/non-recommended classification.

  - Licenses that are popular and widely used or with strong communities

  - Special purpose licenses for organizations, such as governments, that require special conditions

  - Licenses that are redundant with more popular licenses

  - Non-reusable licenses that are specific to their authors and therefore not reusable by others

  - Licenses that have been voluntarily retired

  - Other/miscellaneous licenses that do not fall into any of these categories

Profiting from Open Source

We already briefly discussed the need to correctly choose licenses so that an enterprise can provide differentiation in its products using open source projects. The differentiation piece sets a product apart from other enterprises using the same open source project.

For enterprises to be successful, this differentiation can be made in four broad categories.

Product Contributions

The Android operating system is an excellent example of software under open source license. Many different phone manufacturers use Android. Android's preferred licensing is Apache 2.0, but it also has a Linux kernel and other components on other types of licenses, such as GPL [3-37]. Multilicensing is more of a norm than an exception in the open source world. When making modifications, each phone manufacturer may have to adhere to license policies depending on where the code changes are made. The strategy here could be as simple as building your differentiation in areas of Apache 2.0 license, which applies to the user space where your Android apps live. This strategy is evident to a certain extent when you see the bundled apps from phone manufacturers that come with different phones today. These manufacturer-specific apps may require changes in multiple areas to behave well. Depending on the strict licensing requirements, some of those changes could be contributed back, but others could be made proprietary or only distributable via the manufacturer's marketplace.

Building an Ecosystem

Monetization of open source can also happen by building a unique ecosystem around your open source distribution that other enterprises may not provide.

Tooling used with open source projects is a great example where user experience and preferences can differ significantly. Enterprises can capitalize on these user expectations. Generally, open source software is built to provide one functionality well, leaving a lot to be desired in many other aspects of the software. To benefit from open source software, there are several other ancillary services needed. These include deployment, monitoring as well as management of the software. Tools required for such activities are many times missing or challenging to use. Enterprises could build these tools to provide unique benefits far superior to any current option. Since tooling could be considered a separate project, licensing could be set to whatever serves the creator's best interest.

Open source software contributors typically spend more time on programming than documenting. Enterprises could also provide better documentation that can show their elevated understanding of the open source software, which is likely to attract a lot more users to their distribution of the open source software.

Business Strategies

The right business strategy could help drive tremendous revenue from your open source products. This includes correct product positioning, go-to-market strategy as well partnerships.

Enterprises planning to distribute open source could use their image to their advantage. Here the reputation of the distributor of the software comes into play. Consider this: if an enterprise with excellent security credentials puts its name next to an open source OS distribution, it will likely get more traction with security-minded users.

Enterprises can benefit with the help of their ongoing relationships with their partners and vendors also. Even though various software or even hardware vendors may be contributing code to the open source software, it does not automatically translate to software distribution by each of these vendors. Many vendors may still be interested in partnering. For example, hardware companies shipping their computers to individual users may have several options for bundling applications with them. These applications could be from the enterprises which already have a relationship with these hardware vendors giving them an edge over their other competitors with similar applications.

Enterprises can also target specific users. These could include individual users or companies that do business with them already. These users can be categorized into different types and targeted based on the enterprise's current most extensive user base category.

Product Services

Imagine that you are a user of an open source software that you downloaded and installed yourself. This open source project has millions of lines of code, and contributions come from hundreds, if not thousands, of contributors. Now, if you run into a bug, your options are limited. You could try to fix it yourself, which is highly unlikely since it's a lot of code to understand, and on top of that, open source software licenses provide no warranties. Without any warranty, users would be hesitant to use the software. Enterprises can deliver this extra level of protection to their users by providing a support structure that can resolve any issues within an agreed-upon service level agreement.

Open source software versions change pretty often. Let's say you are not running the latest version of an open source software, and you run into bugs that have been fixed in the latest version. Alternatively, lets say you need a particular feature "that exists or is available" in the latest version of the software only. Both these scenarios require you to upgrade the software.

Upgrades could be a trivial task if you are the only user; however, this could affect an entire organization when there are enterprise users. To complicate matters further, you may have no experience upgrading the software with many users. To handle such scenarios, distributors of open source software can sell upgrade services for their open source software distributions.

Conclusion

It may seem counterintuitive that open source software can be financially beneficial to anyone. We have always believed that patents and copyrights are ideal for any business to protect its intellectual property. However, if you look at some major software products today, they have an open source element. Licensing has not shown to be a severe impediment to open source software acceptance in most cases.

This chapter provided some of the well-known examples of open source licenses. However, as business models change over the years, you can expect these licenses to evolve further or change in relevance. Other categories of licenses, such as Creative Commons [3-38], apply to works other than source code and may apply to organizations depending on various use cases. These can be used for images, music, articles, and so on.

As you begin or continue your journey into open source, remember that your scenario could be unique and may require further understanding before finalizing a license; therefore, consult a lawyer before making any final decisions.

References

[3-1] https://opensource.org

[3-2] www.apache.org

[3-3] https://kubernetes.io/

[3-4] https://source.android.com

[3-5] https://httpd.apache.org

[3-6] https://opensource.org/licenses/
      BSD-3-Clause

[3-7] https://opensource.org/licenses/
      BSD-2-Clause

[3-8] https://go.dev/

[3-9] www.nginx.com

[3-10] www.freebsd.org

[3-11] https://android.googlesource.com/
       platform/bionic/

[3-12] www.gnu.org/licenses/licenses.en.html

[3-13] www.mysql.com

[3-14] https://mariadb.org

[3-15] www.drupal.org

[3-16] https://git-scm.com

[3-17] https://openedx.org/trademark-
       licensing-details/

[3-18] https://opensource.org/licenses/MIT

[3-19] https://github.blog/2015-03-09-open-
       source-license-usage-on-github-com/

[3-20] https://dotnet.microsoft.com/en-us/

[3-21] https://godotengine.org

[3-22] https://keras.io

[3-23] www.tensorflow.org

[3-24] www.lua.org

[3-25] www.putty.org

[3-26] www.mozilla.org/en-US/about/history/

[3-27] www.mozilla.org/en-US/MPL/historical/

[3-28] www.mozilla.org/en-US/firefox/new/

[3-29] www.bugzilla.org

[3-30] www.libreoffice.org

[3-31] www.rabbitmq.com/mpl.html

[3-32] www.eclipse.org/legal/epl-2.0/faq.php

[3-33] www.eclipse.org/ide/

[3-34] www.eclipse.org/che/

[3-35] https://junit.org/junit5/

[3-36] https://opensource.org/
        proliferation-report

[3-37] https://source.android.com/setup/start/
        licenses

[3-38] https://creativecommons.org/about/
        cclicenses/

CHAPTER 4

Securing Open Systems

Security is one of the crucial aspects of the software development process. From conceptualization to a product's release, developers need to ensure that a proactive approach exists to build a secure product. As the software complexity increases, flaws and defects in the software also increase. Bad actors may take advantage of these flaws to exploit the software. Hence security needs to be at the forefront of a software development life cycle.

Security in the Software Development Life Cycle

Each organization has its playbook when it comes to security. To improve security in a product, various mechanisms should be embedded into the software development life cycle (SDLC) (see Figure 4-1).

© Sachin Rathee and Amol Chobe 2022
S. Rathee and A. Chobe, *Getting Started with Open Source Technologies*,
https://doi.org/10.1007/978-1-4842-8127-7_4

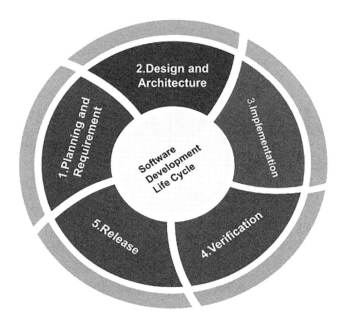

Figure 4-1. *Software development life cycle*

Planning and Requirements

In the traditional SDLC model, the planning and requirement stage gathers all the requirements upfront. This helps finalize the resources and timelines to create the software features needed. Instead of collecting all the requirements upfront, an open source project starts with a high-level idea. This idea leads to the initial implementation of a project released to the community for further evaluation. This is done with minimal planning and resources such that the idea can be first proven as the correct one for wider community acceptance. Ongoing evaluation provides further guidance on additional requirements for future releases. Note that these initial requirements and releases are not meant to be production grade but just to prove the need of the project.

While gathering requirements, it is imperative to think about security along with functionality. It is a good practice to list any security considerations (such as regulatory compliance requirements) along with the functional requirements and employ the right tools to manage such requirements. Open Source Requirements Management Tool (OSRMT) is an open source option that can be used for defining and managing the software requirements [4-1].

Design and Architecture

The design and architecture stage produces a fully developed software design. The *secure by design* paradigm ensures the utmost security and privacy of the software. This approach starts with a robust architecture design, and security is built into the system at every layer. Well-known security strategies are put in place to achieve desired quality. In this phase, software architects work with developers to design the project's overall architecture from functional and non-functional requirements. System engineers ensure all the proper functionality from the requirement phase is addressed, keeping the user experience in mind. Developers participate in open source design communities to understand and improve designs for open source projects. These communities share secure design samples from various open source projects such as Mozilla, Gnome, and Fedora [4-2].

Implementation

The software is developed in the implementation phase. This phase includes software development environment setup, coding, unit testing, and documentation. Before handing over the software to the next phase, developers may demonstrate the functionality to the system engineers to ensure that the software fulfills all the requirements laid out. They also ensure that non-functional requirements like security and usability are addressed properly in this stage. Some of the open source tools that many organizations use to build secure applications include Visual Studio Code [4-3], Budibase [4-4], Vercel [4-5], and Supabase [4-6]. All these tools have integrated security mechanisms or provide the capability to add security plugins that can be used during development.

Verification

Verification is the stage where software is rigorously tested. The quality assurance team tests software from a functionality and deployment point of view and often uses automation tools. Automation helps with the paradigm of test early test often such that issues are caught and fixed early in SDLC. After the QA process, the application goes through a non-functional testing cycle for security, stability, and performance. It verifies that the application continuously performs well and meets service-level agreement (SLA) requirements. There are several open source testing tools available that can help with end-to-end and security testing. Some of the popular ones are Selenium [4-6], Appium [4-7], and Watir [4-8].

Release

The release stage is where the software is generally available (GA) with proper documentation. If any errors or bugs are experienced after the GA, they are reported via customer support. The development teams issue patches for these bugs as part of the patch releases. Open source development follows the "release early, release often" philosophy. In this philosophy, the importance of early and frequent releases is emphasized. This helps create a tight feedback loop between users and developers and provides quick fixes for any security vulnerabilities. This challenges the older philosophy of feature-based releases. Open source tends to follow agile processes for software development due to their iterative/incremental model.

Processes and Tools

SDLC should integrate security-focused continuous delivery mechanisms such as DevSecOps. This can be achieved with specialized tools. These tools reduce risk in development pipelines without slowing down the speed by detecting and fixing security vulnerabilities through continuous security testing. They also allow security teams to oversee the security of development projects without manual review and approval process.

Note   DevSecOps stands for development, security, and operations. Its integrated security is a shared responsibility throughout the software design life cycle.

Since GitHub is the most popular source code repository for open source software, many tools support scanning code directly onto it. Some of the popular examples of DevSecOps tooling which can directly scan projects on GitHub are GitHub Actions [4-9], Trivy [4-10], SonarQube [4-11], and DeepSource [4-12]. DevSecOps tools can be categorized as follows.

- **Static application security testing (SAST)** analyzes source code to detect any traces of vulnerabilities before the code is compiled. Code Warrior is one of the open source tools used for SAST scan [4-13].

- **Dynamic application security testing (DAST)** scans web applications for vulnerabilities. One of the open source tools used for DAST is Zap [4-14].

- **Interactive application security testing (IAST)** combines SAST and DAST to create an interactive application security approach. This interactive approach covers a broader range of code and produces better results due to a holistic view. Contrast is a community edition tool available for IAST scan [4-15].

- **Image scanning** scans containers to identify potential security threats. Clair is one of the popular projects used for static analysis of vulnerabilities in application image containers [4-16].

- **Open source vulnerability scanning** tools check source code for vulnerabilities and security flaws. Some of examples include Metasploit [4-17] , OpenSCAP [4-18], and OpenVAS [4-19].

Open Source Vulnerability Management

According to the National Institute of Standards and Technology (NIST), the definition of *vulnerability* is "a security flaw, glitch, or weakness found in software code that could be exploited by an attacker (threat source)" [4-20]. It's a defect in the program that allows the malicious attacker to gain control of the system. The attacker can then exploit the code vulnerability to compromise sensitive information or install malware or backdoor software. Also, an attacker can use your system to break into another host on the same network. This can cost companies millions of dollars in damages.

A vulnerability can happen because of bad software code or design. The Common Vulnerabilities and Exposures (CVE) program lists publicly disclosed security flaws with a unique identification. The idea behind the CVE program was to create a design where vulnerability databases and associated information are linked together. The CVE program helps corporations, developers, and professionals address these vulnerabilities and make systems more secure. It is overseen by the MITRE Corporation, a non-profit committed to public interests [4-21]. NIST's National Vulnerability Database (NVD) [4-22] is fully synchronized with the CVE; it reports known vulnerabilities that have been assigned CVE unique ids.

Figure 4-2 compares NVD and CVE.

Common Vulnerabilities and Exposures

Common Vulnerabilities and Exposures, is a list of publicly disclosed computer security flaws.

CVE Record Format
• CVE ID number (e.g."CVE-2020-1235" which is PREFIX-YEAR-NUMBERING Format) • Brief description of the security vulnerability. • Any pertinent references (i.e., vulnerability reports and advisories)

NVD Details Content
• CVE ID number • Description • Severity • References to Advisories, Solutions, and Tools • Weakness Enumeration • Known Affected Software Configurations • Change History

National Vulnerability Database

The NVD is the U.S. government repository of standards based vulnerability management data represented using the Security Content Automation Protocol (SCAP).
The NVD includes databases of security checklist references, security-related software flaws, misconfigurations, product names, and impact metrics.

CVE and NVD relationship

The CVE List feeds NVD, which then builds upon the information included in CVE Records to provide enhanced information for each record such as fix information, severity scores, and impact ratings.

NVD also provides advanced searching features such as by OS; by vendor name, product name, and/or version number; and by vulnerability type, severity, related exploit range, and impact.

Figure 4-2. *CVE and NVD mapping*

In 2020 alone, the CVE program identified and cataloged 18,325 vulnerabilities. To rank CVEs, the Common Vulnerability Scoring System (CVSS) is used. Security teams commonly use CVSS scores to prioritize and expedite remediation of vulnerabilities. CVSS provides a calculator and a standard guide to score CVSS vulnerabilities and interpret CVSS scores [4-23].

Many organizations have also published their best practices and approaches for vulnerability disclosure and remediation in open source projects. These can be applied to projects within other enterprises. These include the following.

- Documentation and reporting of securities issues to the project core team.

- Creation of a project core team with resources familiar with identifying the vulnerabilities. The project core team should perform due diligence to determine any application exposure. They should also assess the potential vulnerability impact and decide on the severity for their organization.

- The project core team should proactively work with the developers on patching vulnerabilities and mitigation strategies.

- The project team should engage CVE Numbering Authorities (CNA) to request CVE when a vulnerability is identified. CNA authority should be informed that you are working on the patch such that they can send any embargoed security notification. Embargo notification ensures that bugs are not made public before the fix is ready. Otherwise, customers may be left with publicly disclosed vulnerabilities but no solutions.

- The project core team should have a plan to disclose vulnerabilities publicly. The project maintainer should work with the core team on resolution timelines. Depending on the severity of the vulnerability, the project core team decides whether they want to release a security patch separately to ensure a quick turnaround or release it as a regular patch containing other bug fixes.

Policies and Compliance

Companies who use open source software create a group of stakeholders responsible for designing and maintaining open source software policies for the organization. These policies exist to mitigate any potential risk or legal concerns from using open source software and maximize the impact and benefits of open source software. Before adopting any open source project, policy guidelines must be followed. For example, Red Hat, Inc. publicly offers its open source participation guidelines [4-24].

Typically, a policy for open source projects should include guidance on the following.

- Use of community code

- Contribution to the projects

- Code publishing

- Launch of products with open source components

- Promotion of open source project

- Acceptance of community code

Compliance refers to a company's policies and procedures to meet regulatory or contractual requirements. To ensure adherence, compliance auditing is used. It ensures that an enterprise meets the standards of an industry and is safely operated. The following are some of the common compliance standards.

- **HIPAA** (Health Insurance Portability and Accountability Act of 1996) is a US legislation that provides security provisions for safeguarding medical information [4-25].

- **GDPR** (General Data Protection Regulation) is a data privacy law that sets guidelines for collecting and processing personal information from individuals who live in the European Union [4-26].

- **SOC 2** (System and Organizational Controls) is an internal controls report capturing how a company safeguards customer data [4-27].

- **PCI DSS** (Payment Card Industry Data Security Standard) is an information security standard for corporations that handle branded credit cards [4-28].

- **SOX** (the Sarbanes-Oxley Act of 2002) rules prevent and detect errors in a company's financial reporting process [4-29].

- The **ISO** (International Organization for Standardization) develops quality management standards used by corporations that provide products or services [4-30].

The biggest challenge for any company is to meet these standards without impacting the project timelines and cost of the software development. Many companies rely on automation tools and software to track all the compliance requirements as part of the software development process. Open source tools can help with the compliance and risk management aspects. The following are two of these tools.

- **Eramba** is an open governance, risk, and compliance (GRC) solution. It's a tool that helps with compliance, risk management, control testing, and exception management. Typical use cases for Eramba include SOC 2 compliance, PCI compliance, risk frameworks, vendor assessments, and incident handling [4-31].

- **Comply** is a SOC 2–focused compliance automation tool that focuses on policy generation and ticketing integration [4-32].

Security Organizations

There are many organizations involved in monitoring and building security standards. They help strengthen open source security with the help of communities.

The Open Web Application Security Project (OWASP)

The Open Web Application Security Project (OWASP) [4-33] is a non-profit organization dedicated to web application security. OWASP operates under the open community model and offers videos, tools, projects, and forums to improve web application security.

OWASP describes the top ten concerns for web application security that should be at the forefront of any organization's security policy.

- Broken **access controls** allow attackers to control access to information or functionality to which only privileged users such as administrators or root have access.

- **Cryptographic failures** (previously known as *sensitive data exposure*) occur when an attacker gains access to sensitive data due to vulnerability or cryptography failures; they may sell or utilize it for nefarious purposes.

- **Injection** happens when the malicious attacker injects their own code into a program via exploitation. Some examples are SQL injections, LDAP injections, or command injections.

- **Insecure design** focuses on risks related to design flaws. Introduced in 2021, this requires using more secure design patterns, threat modeling, and reference architecture during the DevSecOps process.

- **Security misconfiguration** is one of the most common vulnerabilities and is usually due to using the default configurations or showing detailed verbose error messages containing secure information.

- **Vulnerable and outdated components**: Libraries and frameworks provide needed functionality that allows developers to avoid redundant work in their web applications. If these reused components are outdated, they may pose security flaws.

- **Identification and authentication failures**: Vulnerabilities in authentication systems typically used for system login can give attackers access to the system and even compromise an entire system using the main admin or root account.

- **Software and data integrity failures** refer to infrastructure and code that fails to protect against integrity violations such as outdated certificates and digital signatures.

- **Security logging and monitoring failures**: Logging and monitoring are pivotal for any application. Most of the applications either do not have an appropriate monitoring structure for the collected critical logs or do not have an automated process of detecting the data breaches. As per the OWASP, the average discovery time for a breach is more than 200 days. This allows the attacker to do more damage before anyone reacts to it.

- **Server-side request forgery** (SSRF) was added based on the industry survey results. SSRF occurs when a web application fetches a remote resource without checking the user-supplied URL. An attacker can compel the application to send a malicious request to an unexpected destination, even when protected by a firewall or VPN.

The Open Source Security Foundation

The Open Source Security Foundation (OpenSSF) seeks to create a future where open source ecosystem contributors use and share secure software [4-34]. OpenSSF focuses on identifying and fixing security vulnerabilities in open source software and developing a suite of tooling, best practices, vulnerability disclosure practices, and research and training. OpenSSF consists of various working groups [4-35] that lead efforts in the following.

- Security tooling

- Securing critical projects

- Identifying security threats

- Digital identity attestation

- Vulnerability disclosures and best practices

As a result of these working groups, OpenSSF manages projects that help the open source community and users understand open source projects' security assessment. These projects help make informed decisions about adopting open source projects based on their security and importance scores. The following are some of these projects.

- **Scorecards** is an automated tool that generates security scores for open source projects that help users understand the risk profile of the open source project [4-36].

- A **criticality score** generates a criticality score for every open source project. Criticality scores define the importance and influence of the project [4-37].

- The **Security Metrics Project** provides security metrics and sustainment information for open source projects [4-38].

- The **Alpha-Omega Project** was launched to proactively find, fix, and prevent vulnerabilities. It has two initiatives: Alpha and Omega. Alpha works with open source project maintainers to look for and address undiscovered vulnerabilities within their project's code. Omega identifies top open source projects to apply automated security analysis, scoring, and remediation guidance [4-39].

- **Sigstore** was created to improve software supply chain integrity and verification. Sigstore makes it easy for developers to sign releases for end users for easy verification [4-40].

Conclusion

There has been a rapid shift to digital technologies in the last decade. Due to the COVID-19 pandemic, this move has been expedited significantly. There are a lot of technical options available for this transition. These options include a plethora of open source projects too. It is important to differentiate and identify the right projects. These projects should be vetted properly, with security being one of the most important aspects.

Only active open source projects with strong community backing see faster security updates. This is possible because, in open source projects, contributors/developers are constantly iterating and releasing new versions. This helps with fixing code bugs and any potential security loopholes quickly.

Awareness around open source security is growing fast. In 2022, The White House held meetings with major hi-tech organization leaders to highlight the need to improve software security and the transparency of the software supply chain [4-41].

References

[4-1] https://github.com/osrmt/osrmt

[4-2] https://opensourcedesign.net/projects/

[4-3] https://github.com/microsoft/vscode

[4-4] https://github.com/budibase/budibase

[4-5] https://github.com/vercel/vercel

[4-6] https://github.com/supabase/supabase

[4-7] http://appium.io

[4-8] http://watir.com

[4-9] https://github.com/features/actions

[4-10] https://github.com/aquasecurity/trivy

[4-11] https://sonarsource.com

[4-12] https://deepsource.io/blog/
hacktoberfest-2020-with-deepsource-
discover/

[4-13] https://github.com/CoolerVoid/
codewarrior

[4-14] www.zaproxy.org/

[4-15] www.contrastsecurity.com/contrast-
community-edition

[4-16] https://github.com/quay/clair

[4-17] https://github.com/rapid7/metasploit-
framework

[4-18] www.open-scap.org

[4-19] www.openvas.org

[4-20] https://csrc.nist.gov/glossary/term/
vulnerability

[4-21] www.mitre.org

[4-22] https://nvd.nist.gov

[4-23] https://nvd.nist.gov/vuln-metrics/cvss/
v3-calculator

[4-24] www.redhat.com/en/resources/
open-source-participation-
guidelines-overview

[4-25]www.hipaa.com

[4-26] https://gdpr.eu

[4-27] https://us.aicpa.org/interestareas/frc/
assuranceadvisoryservices/sorhome

[4-28] www.pcisecuritystandards.org/
document_library

[4-29] www.govinfo.gov/content/pkg/COMPS-1883/
pdf/COMPS-1883.pdf

[4-30] www.iso.org/standards.html

[4-31] www.eramba.org/community-downloads

[4-32] https://github.com/strongdm/comply

[4-33] https://owasp.org

[4-34] https://openssf.org

[4-35] https://github.com/ossf

[4-36] https://github.com/ossf/scorecard

[4-37] https://github.com/ossf/
criticality_score

[4-38] https://github.com/ossf/Project-
Security-Metrics

[4-39] https://openssf.org/community/
alpha-omega/

[4-40] https://github.com/sigstore

[4-41] www.whitehouse.gov/briefing-room/
statements-releases/2022/01/13/readout-
of-white-house-meeting-on-software-
security/

CHAPTER 5

Open Source in Infrastructure

Infrastructure components form the backbone of the information technology stack. Infrastructure can be physical or virtual. A physical infrastructure consists of computers, routers, switches, disks, and so forth. In contrast, a virtual infrastructure divides the physical components into smaller portions and presents them to your software applications. Virtualization software accomplishes this division of physical resources into virtual.

Traditionally, each infrastructure device for storage and networking provided its unique way of configuring and managing. Any changes within the infrastructure setup required touching all the devices separately as there was no centralized control. This individualized control resulted in a lack of a holistic view of the complete networking or storage setup, which are imperative for better security, reduced downtime, and lower setup and debugging costs. Therefore, control and management functionality were decoupled from individual components and moved centrally to achieve higher efficiencies. This paradigm refers to a software-defined approach.

This chapter looks at various open source projects that are relevant to IT infrastructure. It also looks at how software-defined approaches help manage the devices at scale.

© Sachin Rathee and Amol Chobe 2022
S. Rathee and A. Chobe, *Getting Started with Open Source Technologies*,
https://doi.org/10.1007/978-1-4842-8127-7_5

Physical Infrastructure Components

Physical infrastructure components form the foundation for the entire IT stack. The capabilities of this physical stack govern the capabilities of the entire software stack that runs on top of it. The physical components can be categorized as follows.

- **Computing resources** constitute the computers that provide the memory, processing power, local storage, and ability to network via network interfaces which are all critical to running the applications. These computers are usually your PCs and laptops at home, but with data centers, they are called *servers*.

Note   A *data center* is a centralized facility for providing all computing needs for the IT operations of enterprises.

- **Storage systems** hold data for applications. They include hard disks, solid-state drives, and so forth. The storage devices could be local to servers or connected via a network.

- **Network resources** include devices such as routers and switches, which connect remote resources that may not reside within the servers. A simple example would be your home Wi-Fi router that connects all your computers at home. The networking architecture could be much more complex for data centers with multiple routers and switches interconnected to build enough resilience.

Although the open source term has been synonymous with software, open hardware has gained more traction recently. Before delving into the reasons behind this growth, let's discuss what open source hardware implies. Open source hardware deals with the design aspects of hardware components. The main principle here is to allow reuse, modification, and enhancement of the hardware designs by anyone. If any software components accompany the hardware, those components should also be available under open source licenses.

In 2021, the Open Source Hardware Association (OSHWA) [5-1] was formed to provide centralized management of all open hardware-related activities. In 2016, OSHWA started a certification program to ensure that all open hardware conforms to uniform and well-defined standards.

Substantial growth in open source hardware started to show up when existing designs and architecture were not providing enough innovation for the massive scale of IT infrastructure deployed to address the growth of cloud-based services.

Facebook took the lead and brought together a team to specifically rethink its infrastructure. This rethink was triggered by the massive growth of data that Facebook needed to deal with, along with a need to address burgeoning costs and energy consumption in its data centers. None of the existing solutions addressed these issues at the scale that Facebook witnessed. Facebook's goal was to design and develop an efficient data center that can handle the scale of modern applications and data used while keeping the costs associated to a minimum. It spent a couple of years designing the servers, software, power supplies, racks, and cooling from scratch. The final design, when tested, proved to be 24 percent less costly and 38 percent more energy efficient.

After witnessing these positive results, Facebook decided to share its designs publicly in the true spirit of openness to foster further innovation in data center technology. In 2011, Facebook, Rackspace, Goldman Sachs, Intel, and Andy Bechtolsheim formed the Open Compute Project (OCP) [5-2] to share data center components' designs and best practices. This project proved to be a significant catalyst in the open hardware space. There are now close to 50 OCP members. It features a marketplace for OCP-accepted products, OCP-inspired products, or OCP-ready data centers.

OCP-accepted and OCP-inspired products must comply with OCP specifications. OCP-accepted designs are open source for anyone involved. OCP-inspired requires OCP members' involvement. OCP ready is a recognition program for data centers that follow guidelines created by the OCP Data Center Facility Project team.

OCP also features a marketplace [5-3] that allows anyone to view the current products and solutions. It features three categories.

- **Integrated solutions** provide the converged solution stack deployed on the OCP-inspired and OCP-accepted hardware.

- **Products and data centers** include OCP-inspired and accepted products and OCP-ready data centers.

- **Sustainability solutions** include solutions that can be repurposed and reused to reduce waste.

The open hardware movement had few other favorable market conditions beyond Facebook's success. The commoditization of server, storage, and network hardware played an important role. Due to this, hardware products built by one vendor could finally interoperate with hardware products of a different vendor. This interoperability required sharing of specs between vendors. Also, the rise of cloudification, where the cloud providers have much higher purchasing power and thus the ability to influence the future direction of hardware innovation by the vendors, has played a key role.

Finally, the rise of hardware programmability with frameworks such as Open Computing Language (OpenCL) [5-4] has also greatly contributed to the democratization of hardware. Now applications for programmable hardware, such as a field-programmable gate array (FPGA), can be aggregated over marketplaces and shared with anyone easily.

Note   Central processing units (CPUs) are designed to run various general-purpose tasks. They provide ease of programming and can be used for many different use cases. However, their generality leads to performance and cost drawbacks. Performing a repetitive task on a general-purpose CPU seems like a waste. In such scenarios using hardware that does specific repetitive tasks in a much more performant manner makes sense. Specialized hardware such as an *FPGA* help offload these repetitive tasks from CPUs to themselves. They can be programmed to do a specific task well, thus providing better cost and performance.

Provisioning Systems

An operating system is usually the first piece of software deployed on a server as a primary step in building the infrastructure. If you have deployed an operating system on a server, you can imagine the extensive work and steps needed to prep the server. Additionally, diagnostic mechanisms are required to understand any errors during this server provisioning process. If the entire end-to-end provisioning process is done manually, it becomes time-consuming.

Several open source projects help with the automated on-demand deployment and configuration of these servers. They provide the speed and agility needed in any data center environment where there are thousands of servers waiting to be provisioned quickly. Cobbler [5-5] is one such project among many open source options. It uses network boot for the installation process. It also has support for virtual environments as an additional feature.

Virtual Infrastructure Components

While deploying physical infrastructure, you realize that catering to every application's diverse resource, security, architecture, OS supportability, and availability requirements becomes challenging with the same physical infrastructure. Some applications, for example, run better on Linux than others on Windows; some may support easy backup with tools that come with applications, while others may leave that up to the user to define their own backup mechanisms.

Many applications may run securely while sharing resources, while some would require isolation for security or performance. Applications may also differ in architecture, where some applications can run in a distributed fashion, allowing for a larger number of cheaper servers (scale-out model). In contrast, different applications may require a single server with large computing power (scale-up model).

Thinking through these aspects, it becomes clear that if you could partition physical infrastructure into smaller portions and customize it to each application, you can have tremendous flexibility and cost savings. This is indeed the goal of virtualization. Virtualization allows the running of virtual machines, known as *guests* on the physical hosts, through various virtualization techniques. The virtual machines act like a separate physical host, allowing operating systems different from the host to run on them.

Virtualization offers the following benefits.

- The ability to reuse the same physical hardware to emulate different environments without investing in separate hardware.

- Guest applications run on separate guest operating systems providing an extra layer of security between multiple applications and guest and host operating systems.

- Scalability in a distributed fashion.

- Much higher availability and reduced downtime as backing up and re-provisioning of virtual machines are much faster.

- Provides the basis for cloud computing where many resources are pooled for varied applications requirements.

Virtualization Stack

Virtualization is achieved using various mechanisms depending on the end goal. For example, if the end goal is to test your application functionality on different operating systems, the performance may not be a concern. However, if the applications are running in a production environment, you may want to get as much performance from your hardware as possible. Given different use cases for virtualization, multiple modes of virtualization are employed. These modes are full virtualization, paravirtualization, and OS-level virtualization (also known as *containerization*).

Full virtualization requires a hypervisor, also referred to as a *virtual machine monitor* (VMM). A hypervisor is software that runs on physical machines and creates and manages virtual machines. It acts as a translator between physical and virtual resources. Depending on the type of hypervisor, you can achieve software-assisted virtualization/emulation or hardware-assisted virtualization.

A Type 1 hypervisor is the bare metal or native hypervisor because it replaces the host operating system and runs directly on the hardware to achieve hardware-assisted virtualization. It schedules workloads or virtual machines directly on the hardware. For this type of virtualization, hardware-based technologies such as Intel VT and AMD-V (discussed later) are necessary. The Linux kernel-based virtual machine, or KVM [5-6], is an example of an open source Type 1 hypervisor.

Type 2 hypervisors, which are also known as *hosted hypervisors*, require a traditional operating system to run on. Unlike Type 1 hypervisors, which schedule virtual machines on physical hardware, Type 2 schedule VMs on the host operating systems which then interface with hardware. This additional software layer makes this option referred to as *software-assisted virtualization*. Due to this extra software layer, Type 2 is a less performant option than Type 1 hypervisor. An example of an open source Type 2 hypervisor is Quick EMUlator (QEMU) [5-7].

Paravirtualization differs from full virtualization in a critical aspect. In full virtualization, the OS running in a VM (guest OS) has no awareness of virtualization technology in play. The guest OS behaves as if it is running as the host OS. However, in paravirtualization, the guest OS is modified to interface with the hypervisor directly and access the underlying hardware. This improves the performance when compared to full virtualization. However, the need for customized OS reduces the choice of operating systems that can be run on the VMs. KVM with virtIO is an example of paravirtualization.

Typically, a virtual machine is quite heavy in utilizing resources as it runs a complete operating system, the applications, and its dependencies in a single VM. It compensates for this drawback by providing excellent isolation of one VM from another, which helps with greater security. Therefore, a user may have to pick between less resource usage by running as many applications on a single VM and greater security by running each application in its own VM. There is, however, a middle ground. What if you decided to share some standard OS features from the host OS with applications directly without needing a separate guest OS? Additionally, to make the host OS safer, you restrict application access to these shared resources.

To avoid one application hogging all the resources, you control the resources assigned to each application. What we described as *middle ground* is referred to as a *containerized* or *OS-level virtualization solution*.

There is no hypervisor in OS-level virtualization, and applications run in containers instead of VMs. These containers share the host operating system kernel. Examples include LXC (Linux containers) and Docker Engine [5-8]. Figure 5-1 provides a graphical comparison between virtual machines and containers.

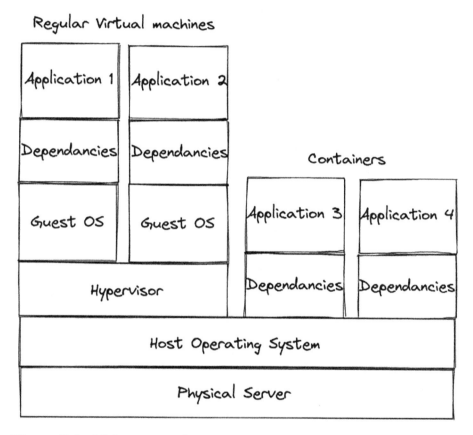

Figure 5-1. *VMs vs. containers*

Let's look at examples of these virtualization stacks in more detail next.

QEMU

QEMU is an open source machine emulator and virtualization software developed by Fabrice Bellard. It emulates a machine's CPU through a dynamic translation of the source instruction set to the target instruction set. It supports different hardware for the machine, enabling it to run various operating systems. QEMU is available under the GPL license.

When it comes to emulation, QEMU supports two emulation modes.

- **Full system emulation** supports the creation of virtual machines which can emulate processors and various peripherals, such as disk, memory, and network cards.

- **User mode emulation**: In this mode, QEMU runs Linux applications compiled for a particular CPU on another underlying CPU by dynamically translating the syscalls. Since the full system is not emulated in this mode, it has many restrictions on capabilities otherwise available on non-emulated systems. For example, the ability to debug an application properly may not be possible. The operating systems supported in this mode are Linux and BSD only.

One of the crucial components of QEMU is the *tiny code generator* (TCG). It is the main binary translation engine that helps with the emulation of CPUs. During emulation, TCG is the one that translates each guest CPU instruction into the host CPU instruction. For virtualization on x86 CPUs architecture, QEMU uses KVM to provide hardware-assisted virtualization. TCG does not come into play in such a scenario as KVM is replaced as the accelerator.

KVM

KVM is the full virtualization solution initially developed in 2006 by Qumranet. Red Hat, Inc. acquired it in 2008. KVM is available under the GPL license. KVM was developed for Linux running on x86 hardware. It requires the support of virtualization extensions within the hardware.

KVM is supported by Intel and Advanced Micro Devices (AMD) hardware. For Intel-based CPUs, it requires Intel VT (Virtualization Technology), and for (AMD) based CPUs, it requires AMD-V (AMD Virtualization). Intel's virtualization technology may serve many use cases, and hence it has different terminology. For example, VT-x represents virtualization technology on the x86 architecture of a CPU (necessary for KVM). VT-i represents IA-64 architecture. KVM architecture requires two components to work: two kernel modules and a user-space module.

Kernel modules provide core virtualization infrastructure and processor-specific drivers. The kernel modules of KVM have been included in mainline Linux distribution since version 2.6.20. The job of the KVM user-space component is to provision and manage virtual machines while communicating with kernel modules. The user-space component is included in the QEMU project, starting with version 1.3.

virtIO

virtIO [5-9] is a virtualization mechanism used with network and disk devices. The initial specification of virtIO was developed by Rusty Russell while at IBM [5-10]. virtIO is available under GPL license within the Linux repository [5-11].

When virtIO is used, the guest operating system is fully aware that it is running on a virtualized setup and therefore falls under the paravirtualization paradigm. virtIO drivers can co-operate with hypervisors such as KVM to optimize the network and disk operations to gain maximum performance. This performance otherwise is not possible in an emulated environment.

libvirt

libvirt [5-12] provides the capability to manage virtualization functionality more conveniently. libvirt is an open source API, daemon and management tool for managing platform virtualization. It helps maintenance of different hypervisors via the same set of tools. libvirt is backed by Red Hat and its initial release was in late 2005.

libvirt offers immense flexibility when building cloud solutions where many hypervisors need to be managed programmatically. libvirt is released under the GNU Lesser General Public License and includes three major components.

- A C language API. However several packages are available that can provide bindings to other languages. These languages include PHP, Perl, Python, Java and Go.

- **libvirtd** is a daemon process running on the server. It performs the management tasks for the virtual machines, such as starting, stopping, migrating and managing storage, and configuring or manipulating networking aspects.

- **virsh** is a command-line utility that implements the libvirt APIs. It communicates with libvirtd to manipulate the virtualized guests or set up configurations.

Linux Containers

Containers may seem like the latest technology in IT. In reality, however, the original idea of containers has been around since the 1970s. This concept was used with Unix systems to provide better security/isolation of applications. Since then, this technology has been going through various iterations and evolutions to better handle the operability of containers.

To better understand container technology, it is important to first understand Linux operating systems. Linux segregates its memory into two areas: *user space* and *kernel space.* The user space is where your/user applications run. The kernel space is much more privileged and allows code execution relating to the kernel functions.

Kernel functions manage the access to the hardware, such as with device drivers. To keep the access to kernel functions secure, only a specific set of APIs are used by the user applications, called *system calls.* These APIs provide guard rails to make sure that the same kernel shared by all applications is not impacted by the actions of any single rogue application. Typically a Linux container would run a single application and use Linux kernel features such as namespaces, SELinux (Security-Enhanced Linux), and secure computing mode (seccomp) to provide application to application and application to kernel level isolation. The resource allocation to each container is managed via cgroups (control groups) limits which is another kernel functionality. This user space and kernel space separation form the basis of containerization. LXC [5-13] is released under GNU Lesser General Public License.

Software-Defined Networking

In traditional networking, it is quite cumbersome to set up networks. Once created, changing the topology would require manually reconfiguring the individual network elements. Even if it was not manual, configuring a network element differed with the vendor and equipment type. Software-defined networking (SDN) aims to change this by centralizing the control plane (the plane which controls how data flows in the network) such that all decisions relating to the network routing can be centralized. SDN aims to use these centralized functions programmatically via well-defined protocols and APIs. This reduces the cost and increases the agility of the networks, and any new services in the network can be provisioned quickly. Let's look at an example of open source implementation of networking components next.

Open Virtual Network

Open Virtual Network (OVN) [5-14] is an SDN solution based on the Open vSwitch (OVS) project (see Figure 5-2) to support virtual network abstraction. It is released under Apache License 2.0.

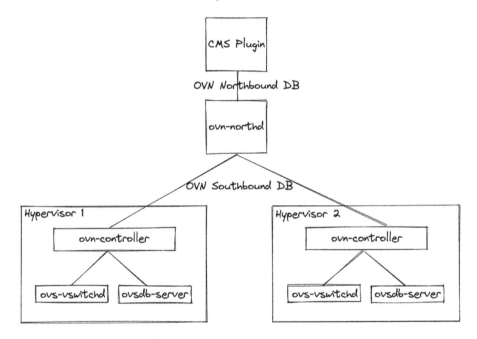

Figure 5-2. *OVN architecture*

OVS is a multilayer virtual switch designed to deploy across multiple physical servers in a distributed fashion. OVN complements OVS by providing logical network abstractions over physical networks. OVN is intended to be used with various *cloud management systems* (CMS) and hence offers plugin-based integration. It primarily consists of the following components.

- **CMS** is the client software that integrates with OVN via a plugin. The first CMS integrated with OVN was OpenStack; however, the Kube-OVN project now intends to replicate a similar type of integration with the Kubernetes platform. Cloud management systems are discussed later.

- **Databases** to store physical and logical network information. It consists of a northbound database that holds the logical network configuration provided by the CMS plugin. A daemon (ovn-northd) translates the logical network configuration in northbound DB into logical data path flows and places them in southbound DB. In addition to the logical network, southbound DB also holds physical network information and bindings that link physical and logical networks together. Hypervisors populate both.

- Various Hypervisors are supported by the OVS project. These hypervisors consist of an ovn-controller agent that learns about configurations and status information from southbound DB and uses that information to control network traffic by connecting with ovs-vswitchd (an OVS component) via OpenFlow protocol. ovsdb-server, an OVS configuration control, and monitoring component, also communicates with the ovn-controller to manage OVS.

- **Gateways** provide a mechanism that allows physical servers to communicate with logical networks.

Software-Defined Storage

Traditionally, the storage solutions were proprietary and monolithic. The storage mechanism could not be separated from the hardware it ran on. Software-defined storage paradigm introduces the ability to separate storage software from the hardware. This allows the software to manage storage on readily available standard hardware such as x86 architecture-based servers. The decoupling also enables scale-out storage on heterogeneous hardware, centralized management, and reduced capital expenditures by avoiding vendor lock-ins. Next, let's look at an example of open source implementation of software-defined storage.

Ceph

Ceph [5-15] is an open source storage platform delivering object, file, and block storage. Sage Weil created it in 2004. In 2012, Weil founded Inktank Storage for professional services and support for Ceph. Red Hat purchased Inktank in 2014. Ceph is released under GNU Lesser General Public License.

Ceph leverages RADOS (Reliable Autonomic Distributed Object Store) to allow the use of commodity hardware and provides a highly reliable and scalable storage mechanism.

To operationalize a Ceph cluster, there are several daemons providing specific functionality needed within the cluster.

- **Monitors**: Monitors maintain maps of the cluster state. These maps allow Ceph daemons to better coordinate among themselves. Monitors also manage authentication between daemons and the clients connecting to the cluster.

- **Managers**: Managers manage runtime metrics and the current state of the Ceph cluster. The metrics include performance metrics, resource utilization, and current load.

- **Object storage daemons** (OSDs) manage data storage, recovery, rebalancing, and replication. They also provide monitoring information to other daemons.

- **Metadata Server** (MDS) comes into play only when a Ceph file system storage is being used and stores metadata on its behalf. Block and object storage do not need MDS.

Cloud Computing

While virtualization is a technology, the cloud is a methodology to deliver virtualized components from a pool of compute, network and storage resources. Now the question becomes, why is this methodology needed? The main reason, of course, is reduced costs. Typically in the virtualized world, it can take months, if not more, to acquire, configure, and provision hardware for use. In cloud computing, the hardware is already available as a pool and can be used on-demand. The automated mechanisms within clouds deploy a virtualized guest per your specification in minutes. This is achieved by making use of pre-created templates provided by cloud providers.

For maximum efficiency in the cloud, applications are expected to be cloud native, which implies that they should be able to utilize all the features and functionality of a cloud. The following are the top three features.

- Lightweight **packaging** with containers.

- **Scale-out functionality** allows applications to run on multiple smaller servers rather than a single high resource server.

- **Stateless** is the ability to run without maintaining a state. If an application goes down, a new application can be spawned up in its place very quickly without losing any in-memory data.

There are two types of clouds: private and public. The private clouds are the ones that service internal enterprise customers. For example, an enterprise may be hosting their cloud in their data center and allowing its use by different internal departments. OpenStack is an example of open source private cloud. On the other hand, public clouds are hosted by independent companies (AWS from Amazon, Azure from Microsoft, Google Cloud from Google), and they sell their cloud services to other enterprises. Since the infrastructure is available to anyone, these clouds are named public clouds. When clouds offer a service that provides the infrastructure to its users, it's called *infrastructure as a service* (IaaS).

Clouds require centralized management via their control plane. The control plane runs the software for managing and controlling each of its services. Networking and storage, two of the cloud's primary services, can benefit immensely by employing software-defined architecture. This is the main reason why software-defined storage and software-defined networking are part of the cloud architectures. Let's look at the open source examples of cloud technologies.

OpenStack

OpenStack [5-16] is an open source cloud platform that provides applications with on-demand, virtualized, containerized, and bare-metal resources. It began in July 2010 as a joint project of NASA and Rackspace. The first version of OpenStack was released in October 2010. OpenStack is available under Apache License 2.0.

OpenStack is primarily used as an IaaS platform. OpenStack is designed in a modular fashion containing several services working together. Each of these services represents different types of resources.

Users can request these resources via service APIs. The following are Openstack's primary services which provide specific capabilities listed.

- **Nova** is the compute service for OpenStack. It provides virtual machine creation and termination. Nova uses different supported hypervisors. It can support QEMU/KVM and Xen.

- **Neutron** enables network connectivity between VM instances. It uses SDN technologies such as OVN for this purpose.

- **Cinder** provides block storage for OpenStack. It exposes the block devices to virtual instances. Cinder supports several backend drivers, including Ceph RBD. Ceph is discussed later in the chapter.

- **Swift** provides the object storage service for OpenStack. This is comparable to the S3 service on AWS. Ceph's RadosGW can be used with swift as a backend to store the unstructured data, which can later be accessed via Restful APIs.

- **Horizon** provides the dashboard for OpenStack. It can be used to visualize and maintain the life cycle of various services provided by OpenStack.

- **Glance** provides services that include managing and retrieving cloud images for virtual machines. VM images can be stored in diverse storage systems, varying from file systems to object storage systems.

- **Keystone** provides authorization and authentication services. Keystone can be integrated with different identity systems, such as the Lightweight Directory Access Protocol (LDAP).

Kubernetes

Kubernetes [5-17] is a container orchestration platform primarily providing *container as a service* (CaaS) to its users. It is released under Apache License 2.0. Initially developed by Google, it was open sourced in 2014 and is now part of Cloud Native Computing Foundation (CNCF). CNCF hosts many open source infrastructure-related projects. It is part of the Linux Foundation. Today, close to 1,000 enterprises contribute to the Kubernetes platform and various individual projects within it.

Kubernetes architecture is divided into control plane components and worker node components. Control plane components make centralized decisions relating to the overall cluster. These include scheduling and detecting and responding to events within the cluster. Worker nodes host user applications (also known as *pods*) and provide them with the runtime environment.

The following are the main control plane components.

- **kube-apiserver** exposes the Kubernetes API. Kubernetes is quite API-centric. Communication with various Kubernetes components is done via APIs.

- **etcd** is the database that holds the state within the Kubernetes cluster. For high availability purposes, etcd should be properly replicated and backed up.

- **kube-scheduler** assigns resources to new workloads being scheduled. It uses various policies to make the correct worker node assignment.

- **kube-controller-manager** runs various controller processes. The controller processes are code logics that look for events in the cluster and move the cluster to the desired state based on these events.

- **cloud-controller-manager**: The Kubernetes cluster can run on virtual machines in the cloud and directly on bare metal. In cases where Kubernetes is running on a cloud, this component runs a controller specific to that cloud.

The following are worker node components.

- **kubelet** runs where pods are running and makes sure that the pods are healthy.

- **kube-proxy** helps with the network communication between the pods. It maintains the network rules that allow communication to your pods from network sessions inside or outside your cluster.

- The **container runtime** is responsible for running containers. Kubernetes supports different container runtimes via a well-defined interface. Open source runtime examples include Docker, CRI-O, and containerd.

Management and Orchestration

Management and orchestration systems can automate the life cycle of the individual infrastructure components (such as cloud resources, including VMs, storage, etc.) and the applications running on top. Once the applications are deployed, day-to-day management is also handled by these management and orchestration systems in an automated fashion. These functions include scaling, closed-loop automation, application and infrastructure updates, and upgrades. ManageIQ [5-18] is an example of an open source tool that can manage and orchestrate both virtualized and containerized solutions.

Conclusion

The end-to-end architecture based on open source infrastructure is represented in Figure 5-3. The bare metals provisioning tools like Cobbler help deploy the operating system on the machines shown in Figure 5-3. That is usually followed by deploying control and data planes for virtualization or cloud systems such as OpenStack or Kubernetes on the operating system, and this forms the cloud layer. The control plane manages the cloud services and ensures high availability, while the data plane provides computing, network, and storage for the application workloads. The network component can be OVN-based, while storage can be based on Ceph.

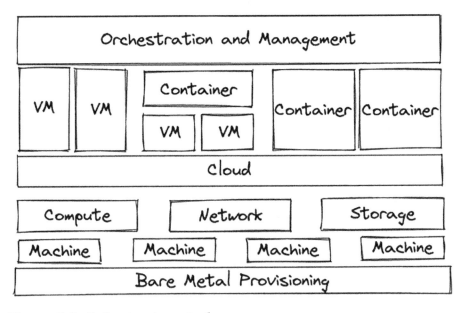

Figure 5-3. *Infrastructure stack*

This two-step process is usually replaced by using specific installation modules that take care of bare-metal provisioning and cloud deployment in a single step. In OpenStack, the TripleO project [5-19] is an example of such an installer.

Once the cloud software is deployed, the orchestrations and management systems can deploy the workload on top of it as VMs and/or containers based on application requirements. This environment can be further scaled on-demand with the help of management and orchestration systems.

References

[5-1] www.oshwa.org

[5-2] www.opencompute.org

[5-3] www.opencompute.org/products

[5-4] www.khronos.org/opencl/

[5-5] https://cobbler.github.io

[5-6] www.linux-kvm.org

[5-7] www.qemu.org

[5-8] https://docs.docker.com/engine/

[5-9] https://wiki.libvirt.org/page/Virtio

[5-10] https://ozlabs.org/~rusty/virtio-spec/
virtio-paper.pdf

[5-11] https://github.com/torvalds/linux/tree/
master/drivers/virtio

[5-12] https://wiki.libvirt.org

[5-13] https://linuxcontainers.org

[5-14] www.ovn.org

[5-15] https://ceph.com

[5-16] www.openstack.org

[5-17] https://kubernetes.io

[5-18] www.manageiq.org

[5-19] https://wiki.openstack.org/wiki/TripleO

CHAPTER 6

Open Source Software for Emerging Technologies

This chapter discusses the use of open source software in emerging technologies such as artificial intelligence (AI), machine learning (ML), and the Internet of Things (IoT). It explains the concepts behind AI, ML, and IoT and lists some of the important projects in each. Then you learn about their adoption within different industries.

What Are AI, ML, DL, and IoT?

Artificial intelligence is all about training machines to adapt human behavior and thinking abilities. It allows machines to perform tasks that humans usually perform. Let's look at a centralized grocery market sorting center where objects like milk, juice, and water are sorted based on their labels. Here AI is used to perform predefined tasks with the help of a rule-based algorithm. This example shows how AI can help improve the speed and accuracy of mundane tasks.

© Sachin Rathee and Amol Chobe 2022
S. Rathee and A. Chobe, *Getting Started with Open Source Technologies*,
https://doi.org/10.1007/978-1-4842-8127-7_6

Machine learning applies AI. According to IBM, "Machine learning is a branch of artificial intelligence and computer science which focuses on using data and algorithms to imitate the way that humans learn and, gradually improving its accuracy" [6-1].

Our previous example of AI had a limitation. The sorting was based on the labels of the objects, and if a label was incorrect, the object would be placed in the wrong bin. Yet, ML starts with creating a blueprint based on the features/attributes of an object. Feature extraction logic helps to differentiate the objects based on the color or size of the container and trains the model with known data sets to build the algorithm that differentiates between the objects. In our previous example, it would mean identifying milk from the color white and packaged in a one-gallon container vs. water that is colorless and in a smaller bottle. With this newly trained model, the system can sort based on the object's characteristics and not rely on labels.

Note   Feature extraction reduces the total number of features in a data set. This is achieved by creating new features from the existing ones. Old features may be discarded as these new features summarize the information from the original set of features.

Deep learning (DL) goes a step further into ML. It is a subset of machine learning that teaches computers to do what comes naturally to humans when dealing with a very large set of data. Compared to ML, DL doesn't necessarily need tagged images to classify the objects into several categories. It can deduce the correct category based on the vast amount of data used to build its model.

Let's further expand on our last example where the use case is changed to sort the objects that the ML model is not already trained on. This could mean adding additional drinks to the current set of milk, juice, and water. Deep learning is then used to train the model with many different images of various objects, which may not be limited to drinks or objects under consideration. This mechanism teaches the model what each object looks like based on the size of containers, color, the material of packaging, labels, and so forth. Each image goes through the different layers of analysis within the DL model, and in the process, each layer sorts objects based on different features of the objects. This type of analysis and sorting needs a lot of data and the computational power to create the appropriate model.

The evolution of AI/ML/DL is considered an industrial revolution powered by the Internet of Things (IoT) and the cloud. IoT is a trend where many devices employ communication services offered by Internet protocols to interconnect. IoT integrates day-to-day "things" with the internet. Data plays a large role, and it links all these technologies together by allowing AI/ML/DL to make decisions based on the data patterns that it receives from IoT devices. Many of these devices, often called "smart objects," are not directly operated by humans but exist as components in buildings or vehicles or are spread out in the environment [6-2]. With the emergence of inexpensive computer chips and reliability and improvisation of the bandwidth in telecommunication, there is tremendous growth in the IoT domain. The following are some IoT examples.

- In big cities, parking can be a huge problem. This problem can be mitigated with IoT sensors attached to parking lots to detect parked cars and send data over clouds to identify vacant parking spaces close to the driver's proximity.

- Waste management companies use IoT sensors to continuously monitor the fill levels of the conventional bins and send the data to the waste management department to efficiently manage the pickup schedule.

- IoT sensors can manage water levels in central water towers by sending alerts to the homeowner or concerned authority regarding the water levels. This helps with water conservation.

Figure 6-1 shows the visual representation of AI/ML/DL and its relationship to IoT. Major IoT vendors are now offering Integrated AI capabilities that simulate smart behavior. A good example of AI-powered IoT is Nest's smart thermostat. It can self-learn the occupants' behaviors and adjust temperatures for different times of the day.

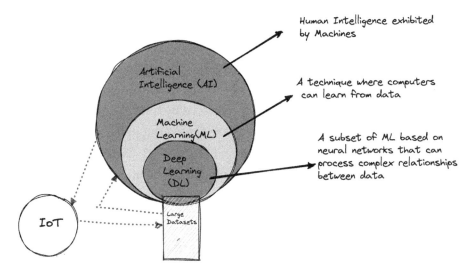

Figure 6-1. *A visual representation of AI, ML, and DL*

Artificial Intelligence Implementation

AI/ML workflow is a sequence of tasks that run in a machine learning implementation. These workflows can vary by project and help define which phases are implemented in a project. The following describes these phases, which are also illustrated in Figure 6-2.

1. **Data preparation** involves the collection and digitization of the data. After collecting all the data, it's formatted and cleaned. Finally, this data is selected as a sample. This stage is critical in ensuring that the data set is fair since the study is based on this data. There are different alternative techniques to prepare data, including extract transform load (ETL) batch processing, data wrangling, and streaming ingestion. The best techniques are selected based on a use case. One of the open source tools used for this stage is KNIME [6-3].

2. **Transformation** of the data helps to harmonize data that may have been initially acquired in various sizes and formats. Data passes through a list of alterations in this process. After removing any anomalous values generated by errors, it is acquired from various sources and then organized into a single data set. You then label it and enhance the data by removing any potential duplicates so that data is ready for the training process. There are open source projects like OpenRefine, which help with disparate data. It cleans and transforms it into a single format. It can also link and extend your data set with various web services [6-4].

3. **Training** involves evaluating the data set, which is now well-formatted and organized. This step goes through different training algorithms to learn appropriate parameters and features to classify the data set. Training the data is a long process of teaching the model to perform desired AI tasks. Repetitive steps are executed on data using mathematical functions to get the desired results with a high level of probability. These mathematical functions are then modified, updated, and repeated until a high level of accuracy is achieved. There are a lot of frameworks available for this task, which you will learn later in the chapter.

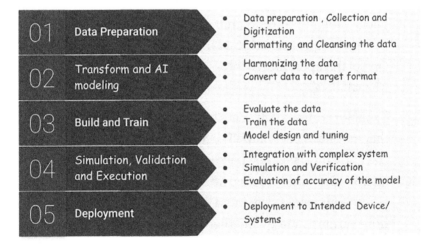

01	Data Preparation	• Data preparation , Collection and Digitization • Formatting and Cleansing the data
02	Transform and AI modeling	• Harmonizing the data • Convert data to target format
03	Build and Train	• Evaluate the data • Train the data • Model design and tuning
04	Simulation, Validation and Execution	• Integration with complex system • Simulation and Verification • Evaluation of accuracy of the model
05	Deployment	• Deployment to Intended Device/ Systems

Figure 6-2. *AI ML workflow*

4. **Simulation, validation, and execution** are where the model is then integrated with a complex system to do the simulation and verification tests. These tests are repeated till it provides a consistent result,

and all tests are fully validated in the system. The model's accuracy is then evaluated based on the consistency of the desired output.

Tests are then done using an inference process to ensure desired outputs are consistent with the training model output. The inference process uses a trained model to make predictions against the previously unseen data. Here live data points are fed into machine learning algorithms. The inference process is done in real-time. Figure 6-3 shows the training vs. inference process. A great example of this process is the Uber Eats app, where Uber uses the power of inference to predict the time for food delivery [6-5].

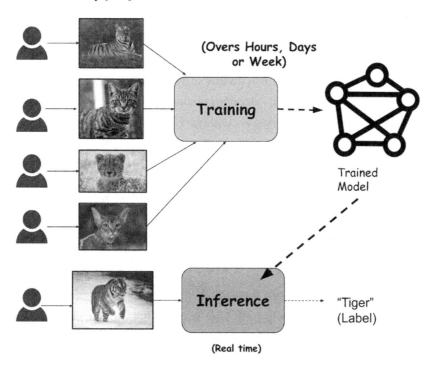

Figure 6-3. *Training vs. inference*

5. **Deployment** of the model on the intended device is the final step. Here you see how the model performs after the deployment. If needed, you may have to revisit the steps done with new data sets and or new characteristics to train the model. One of the popular tools for deployment purposes is TensorFlow Serving [6-7].

AI Engine Framework and Tooling

With predictive analysis (a way to predict future incidents or events based on past behavior), AI companies focus on a data-driven strategy. Companies accumulate large amounts of data and require tools and technology to analyze this data. That is where the AI engine and framework come into the picture. An AI framework, along with various low-level/high-level programming languages and tools, allows companies to expedite creating artificial intelligence applications that can provide valuable business insights. These business insights can drive companies on higher growth trajectories. According to an August 2021 survey by Illuminas, 65 percent of enterprises will use open source technology for AI/ML by 2023 [6-6].

Note   Low-level languages are programming languages that have better performance due to the programmer or a developer making many decisions and optimizing the code. C and C++ are examples of low-level languages.

A high-level language offers a series of abstractions as compilers decide on the developer's behalf. This is not efficient from the code execution point of view because a decision made by compilers may not be optimal for your use case. However, the more significant trade-off is it helps in expediting the time to develop the code. Python and JavaScript are examples of high-level languages.

The following are some of the most popular open source frameworks.

- **TensorFlow** was developed by Google Brain, the company's AI research team, for internal use in 2015. Google then made it open source to accelerate research on machine learning. It is a complete end-to-end open source platform for machine learning. Its main aim is to simplify the process of creating machine learning models. It uses visual models and flowgraphs, which helps developers create machine learning models leveraging data easily. TensorFlow contains libraries, tools, and community resources [6-7].

- **Neo-AI is** Amazon's open source SageMaker Neo project. It uses machine learning models and allows them to run anywhere in the cloud. The Neo-AI project is focused on edge computing and IoT sensors where low latency is the key. Developers and hardware vendors use Neo-AI to customize applications and hardware platforms by taking advantage of Neo's reduced resource usage techniques and optimization features [6-8].

- **Keras** provides a high-level machine learning API that can run on top of the TensorFlow Developer experience, and simplicity makes Keras the go-to project for rapidly prototyping new apps. Keras's interface makes learning and writing the machine learning models much easier than TensorFlow.

However, simplicity sacrifices some performance and speed but makes up for the time needed to create the models. Keras is also released by Google and is open source [6-9].

- **Theano** is a numerical computation library that defines, optimizes, and evaluates complex mathematical expressions involving multidimensional arrays. Theano can run effectively on a CPU and a GPU. The computations in Theano are similar to the NumPy format. It is considered a low-level framework [6-10].

- **PyTorch** is a machine learning framework developed by Facebook and popular in *natural language processing* (NLP) and computer vision applications. It uses dynamic computations graphs. PyTorch is deeply integrated with Python, and you can take advantage of the Python debugging mechanism for it [6-11].

- The **Microsoft Cognitive Toolkit** (CNTK) is a deep learning framework. CNTK supports various languages such as Python, C++, C#, and Java. It acts as a library in the project. Brands such as Skype, Bing, and Cortana, which have massive data sets and require a scalable and highly optimized machine learning platform, use CNTK as a framework. Microsoft has not released any new updates to CNTK since 2019, so CNTK is considered deprecated [6-12].

Note   Python is the most popular language for developers embarking on their AI journeys.

In addition to the frameworks mentioned, there are a lot of other open source projects that machine learning enthusiasts can contribute to and can take advantage of. Open source AI projects may include reference architectures, data sets, predefined algorithms, and readily available interfaces. The following are some of the projects.

- **Analytics Zoo** is an open source project by Intel analytics that provides the big data AI platform with capabilities that helps scale AI to distributed big data. One of the biggest challenges for a data scientist is to apply deep learning to big data pipelines since this requires integrations of many separate components of the big data world like Apache Spark, TensorFlow, Apache HDFS, and so forth. This can be very complex and time-consuming. (A data pipeline includes processes and various tools that help in automating the transformation and movement of data between a source system and a target repository.)

  Analytics Zoo addresses that problem. Analytics Zoo seamlessly brings TensorFlow, Keras, Spark, and BigDL into an integrated pipeline that can scale to large spark clusters for distributed training and inference [6-13].

- **Caliban** is a machine learning project from Google. It is often challenging for the developers working on data science projects to build an environment or a testbed where they can mimic the real-world scenario, and it's impossible to foresee all types of edge cases. Caliban solves that problem by allowing the development of any machine learning model, running the code locally, and then using the power of the cloud environment to execute on a large, powerful machine. Caliban executes its code in an isolated and reproducible docker environment [6-14].

- **Kornia** allows classical computer vision to be integrated into deep learning models in the form of a library. This project started as a small package and eventually became a Kornia project. It inherited the main PyTorch features. Kornia is essentially a computer vision library that consists of a set of routines and modules to solve generic computer vision problems. It is available on GitHub and can be installed on any Linux, macOS, or Windows operating system. PyTorch is a single dependency to run Kornia [6-15].

- **Dopamine** is an open source project by Google. It is a TensorFlow-based research project that is used for the fast prototyping of reinforcement learning algorithms. Reinforcement learning is part of machine learning, where the machine learns through trial and error. This project targets users interested in speculative research experimentation [6-16].

- **DeepDetect** contains a machine learning API and a server. It focuses on simplicity, ease of use, and integration with existing applications. This project trains and manages different deep learning models [6-17].

- **MLJAR** is an automated machine learning tool that builds several models based on a selected algorithm and gets the final predictions. It provides model visualization once the training is done [6-18].

- **LF AI & Data** was founded by the Linux Foundation to create a sustainable AI ecosystem using open source technologies. There are many projects which are part of this ecosystem [6-19].

- **Open Data Hub** is based on Red Hat learnings from internal AI/ML initiatives. It is a reference architecture based on open source community projects such as PyTorch, Apache Spark, JupyterHub, Seldon, Apache AirFlow, and KubeFlow. The deployment of various components is fully automated with an Open Data Hub Kubernetes operator. It is a meta-project that integrates open source projects into a practical solution [6-20].

IoT devices enhanced with the power of AI and ML open source projects are evolving faster. The following are some of the projects that are active in this domain.

- **M2MLabs Mainspring** is an open source application framework that allows building machine-to-machine applications. It is based on Apache Cassandra, a NoSQL database, and Java. It is often used for fleet management and remote monitoring [6-21].

- **Thinger.io** is a cloud IoT platform that helps streamline the development of IoT projects by providing tools that help prototype and manage the IoT device. It is an open source platform; however, it also provides the ready-to-use cloud infrastructure for IoT for a fee [6-22].

- **ThingsBoard** is an open source IoT platform for collecting data, processing data, visualization, and device management. This platform supports on-premises as well as cloud infrastructure. This allows you to regulate remote devices by allowing access to a real-time dashboard [6-23].

- **OpenRemote** is an open source IoT platform that provides users the flexibility to create customized IoT applications. This project provides a dashboard that is used to manage the configuration and behavior of the applications easily by creating specific rules [6-24].

- **DeviceHive** is an open source platform that provides the ability to bootstrap the development of home automation, telemetry, smart energy, and monitoring software. This platform can integrate with many devices using a wide variety of supported protocols [6-25].

Hardware for AI/ML/IoT Workloads

While some projects help you kick start your AI-driven project on a laptop or desktop, specialized hardware is often needed to handle a workload during the training phase or a production run. The best hardware depends on the type of operation and data set. Choosing the right hardware greatly impacts the performance of the machine learning model.

AI and ML have been instrumental in accelerating the development of smart applications, and these applications are increasing in complexity. Semiconductor companies continue to develop powerful processors and accelerators and CPUs, TPUs, and GPUs to keep up with the demands of these applications.

A CPU is central to all the AI workload, whether handling the entire workload or partnering with a co-processor. A graphics processing unit (GPU) is a dedicated processor that operates along with the CPU and acts as a performance accelerator. A GPU is commonly used to run multiple parallel tasks, including graphics processing, machine learning, video rendering, and mining cryptocurrency.

In May 2016, Google designed a tensor processing unit (TPU) to perform fast dense vector and matrix calculations (as part of linear algebra) for neural network machine learning acceleration on TensorFlow software. TPU is an ASIC (application-specific integrated circuit). Deep learning models that take weeks to train on the GPU now take only hours on the TPU.

Note   Neural networks reflect the behavior of the human brain. Using a computer algorithm, neural networks can recognize hidden patterns and correlate the raw data. Neural networks can assess many different types of input, including images, videos, files, databases, and more, and can be applied to a broad range of problems.

Field programmable gate arrays (FPGAs) are integrated circuits with programmable hardware fabric. They provide the ability to customize processing operations in the field/site. This allows AI devices to be more adaptable to changes in requirements.

Figure 6-4 compares the chips discussed in the context of AI.

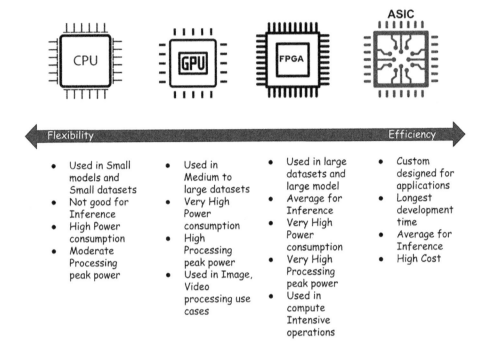

Figure 6-4. *CPU, GPU, FPGA, and ASIC usage and differentiation*

The latest hardware options for AI include tinyML, Glow, and Apache TVM.

tinyML [6-26] is very energy efficient compared to CPU, GPU, and TPU, making it ideal for ML applications running on the edge. Arduino, which is an open source hardware company, released tinyML. tinyML's main focus is optimizing ML workload to be processed on small devices.

Glow was started by Meta in a partnership with industry stalwarts like Intel, Marvell (now owned by Nvidia), and Cadence. Glow is a machine learning compiler and execution engine that runs on heterogeneous hardware, including next-generation machine learning accelerators. Glow accelerates the performance of a deep learning framework [6-27].

Tensor Virtual Machine (TVM) is an open deep learning compiler stack to compile various deep learning models [6-28]. Apache TVM is an open source machine learning compiler framework for CPUs, GPUs, and ASICs. It aims to optimize and improve computational efficiency on any hardware platform. TVM can compile deep learning models into minimum deployable modules suitable for any device.

How Businesses Use AI, ML, and IoT

Many enterprises are using AI and ML to improve various facets of businesses. Retail industries rely on AI for automated chatting via text to speech technologies. This increases overall customer satisfaction by giving customers access to requested information quickly and avoids the usual long wait times for a live human agent to come on a call and address any concerns. Another example is the banking industry, which relies on artificial intelligence for fraud analysis or portfolio recommendations. ML models analyze huge data sets from different streams using very complex algorithms to identify patterns. These patterns help to predict and respond to any fraudulent situation. The International Data Corporation (IDC) expects US enterprises to spend more than $120 billion on AI by 2025 [6-29].

AI and ML make IoT more valuable by making devices and resulting services more intelligent. One of the best examples of IoT that you see in day-to-day life is in cars, where parents can track children's driving behaviors or vehicles that can automatically notify the authorities of an accident, or insurance companies that can monitor the client's driving behavior to give them better rates.

AI and ML have the potential to enhance all aspects of a business by helping achieve measurable outcomes in the following areas.

- Improving the business services by predicting consumer purchasing habits and market trends. This helps businesses to make informed decisions and provide customized services for the consumer.

- Automating operations by streamlining mundane and repetitive tasks. This saves both time and resources.

- Reducing the cost involved with a live person by applying modern AI back technologies like natural language AI chatbot. This also improves the customer experience because as wait times can be significantly reduced.

- Enhancing risk management by using AI applications for IoT. This helps better understand and predict a variety of risks that can be remediated with automated rapid response. Some examples include better worker safety management, predicting auto driver insurance premiums based on their driving patterns, and detecting fraudulent behavior at bank ATMs.

AI, ML, and IoT Use Cases

Industries have many use cases that AI/ML and IoT can address. Some of these use cases may be common to all industries, while many are specific to a particular industry. Let's check out the examples of a few use cases used in the industries today.

Life Sciences and Healthcare Industries

AI is helping the life sciences and healthcare industries be more personalized in engaging with medical professionals and patients. AI has enhanced everything from clinical trial data flow to self-healing applications. The following are some use cases.

- AI chatbots assist doctors in diagnosis and prescription management.

- An AI-based audit system to minimize prescriptions errors.

- Detailed analytics of patient data collected by sensors to generate deep insights into health and find real-time case prioritization and triage.

- Best-personalized treatment plans according to patient data to increase effectiveness.

- Precision-level surgery procedures by robots.

- Detecting diseases like cancer early by finding patterns using medical imaging.

- Gene analysis for drug discovery.

- Customer experience improvements in the hospital industry.

- Automation of the entire clinical trials process to reduce the trial cycle time.

Some of the open source projects in this area are Monai and Healthcare.AI. Monai is a framework for deep learning in healthcare imaging [6-30]. Healthcare.AI is a predictive analytics software [6-31].

Insurance

AI is reshaping the insurance industry by making better, faster, data-driven decisions and streamlining claims processing. The following are some use cases.

- Automates claims processing and appeal processing to reduce time

- Uses onboard diagnostics IoT devices to understand driving patterns to determine insurance premiums

- Recognizes accident images and estimates the repair cost in real-time

- Tailors personalized services and round-the-clock support by AI

- Offers anomaly detection and fraud detection in the insurance industry

One open source project in this sector is open Insurance Data Link (openIDL). It is an open blockchain network that streamlines regulatory reporting and provides insights [6-32].

Automobile

AI is the backbone of the automobile industry for self-driving and connected cars and is helping in reshaping the automobile industry. The following are some of the use cases.

- Driver assistance and safety by providing alerts and warnings in automobiles

- Car manufacturing unit cuts down costs from the prototyping to the testing stage with the creation of smart factories

- Complex supply chain vendor management

- Analysis of dealership data to better understand the supply and demand of vehicles

- Building automated cars by combining powers of sensor types, like radar, cameras, and Light Detection and Ranging (LiDAR)

Two open source projects in this sector are AGL (Automotive Grade Linux), which focuses on a fully open software stack for the connected car [6-33], and OpenPilot, which focuses on driver assistance systems [6-34].

Financial Services

Financial services use AI to improve and modernize offerings by gaining more valuable insights based on the data collected from consumers. It is also helping them to enhance cybersecurity and improve internal process efficiency. The following are other use cases.

- Credit card fraud detection

- Money laundering detection

- Investment predictions based on market insights and real-time changes in specific markets

- Wearable devices to ease the transaction for customers

- Algorithm trading to make better and real-time trading decisions

- Financial advice based on the spending pattern

- Robo-advisors create portfolios and advice on trading, investment, and retirement plans

Two open source projects in this sector are Perspective, an analytics and data visualization component for large data sets and/or streaming data sets [6-35], and Compliant Financial Infrastructure, which focuses on the adoption of the services that meet regulatory and internal security controls for hyperscalers [6-36].

Telecommunications

There are many telecom domain-specific use cases where AI transforms communications reliability, including the following.

- Network anomaly detection to detect slowdown and optimize network performance

- Fault detections and fault predictions, along with finding an optimal resolution

- Network planning and network upgrades

There are organizations in the telecom sector leveraging open source projects to aid telco-specific use cases, such as the Telecom Infra Project [6-37] and the Open Networking Foundation [6-38].

Energy

The energy sector uses AI to perform predictive maintenance and better understand supply and demand. The following are some of the use cases.

- Using a smart grid to learn and adapt based on the energy requirements and improve the energy efficiency of a smart grid

- AI-backed sensors that help the energy sector from unplanned downtimes.

- Detecting defects in fault susceptible processes like wiring/pipes/machines.

- AI tools to encrypt power grids to protect them from
  cyber attacks

The Linux Foundation's LF Energy project is focused on several open
source projects for the energy sector. A popular one is Grid eXchange
Fabric (GXF), an IoT platform that allows grid operators to run smart
devices on the grid [6-39].

Conclusion

AI/ML offers many advantages that help increase customer satisfaction,
automate mundane tasks, and increase a business's top line. AI/ML
technology is no longer a nice to have technology but a necessity of the
time for the enterprises to stay in the competition. AI as a service is also
becoming popular, allowing companies to experiment with AI with lower
risk and without a huge investment.

This domain of AI/ML is still evolving, and many new use cases are
emerging. Open source plays a big role in this by providing a framework
and new projects driving this innovation. Companies are relying on the
power of communities and even releasing closed systems to open source
communities. As an example, Microsoft has open sourced SynapseML,
previously known as MMLSpark, which simplifies the creation of the ML
pipeline [6-40].

Data is one of the core business assets. The more data you collect, the
more advantages you can leverage different learning models from AI/ML
to understand various business patterns. While choosing the tools for AI,
data scientists focus on interoperability (using the same tools for various
types of data) and collaboration (having tools centralized rather than each
working in isolation) as the key factors to increase productivity and make
better use of IT resources.

In the world of IoT, many innovations are emerging. Real-time data from various sensors within devices can now be collected. This collected information can be used with AI-enabled decision-making to develop insights and specific actions.

References

[6-1] `www.ibm.com/cloud/learn/machine-learning`

[6-2] `https://datatracker.ietf.org/doc/html/rfc7452`

[6-3] `www.knime.com/gather-wrangle`

[6-4] `https://openrefine.org`

[6-5] `https://eng.uber.com/uber-eats-trip-optimization/`

[6-6] `www.redhat.com/rhdc/managed-files/rh-enterprise-open-source-report-f27565-202101-en.pdf`

[6-7] `www.tensorflow.org`

[6-8] `https://github.com/neo-ai`

[6-9] `https://keras.io`

[6-10] `https://thirdeyedata.io/theano/`

[6-11] `https://pytorch.org`

[6-12] `https://docs.microsoft.com/en-us/cognitive-toolkit/`

[6-13] `https://github.com/intel-analytics/analytics-zoo`

[6-14] `https://github.com/google/caliban`

[6-15] https://github.com/kornia/kornia

[6-16] https://github.com/google/dopamine

[6-17] https://github.com/jolibrain/deepdetect

[6-18] https://github.com/mljar/mljar-supervised

[6-19] https://lfaidata.foundation/projects/

[6-20] https://opendatahub.io

[6-21] https://sourceforge.net/p/m2mlabs/wiki

[6-22] https://github.com/thinger-io

[6-23] https://github.com/thingsboard

[6-24] https://github.com/openremote

[6-25] https://github.com/devicehive

[6-26] https://github.com/mit-han-lab/tinyml

[6-27] https://github.com/pytorch/glow

[6-28] https://github.com/apache/tvm

[6-29] www.idc.com/getdoc.jsp?containerId=prUS48958822

[6-30] https://monai.io

[6-31] https://healthcare.ai/

[6-32] https://openidl.org

[6-33] www.automotivelinux.org

[6-34] https://github.com/commaai/openpilot

[6-35] https://github.com/finos/perspective

[6-36] https://github.com/finos/compliant-financial-infrastructure

[6-37] https://telecominfraproject.com/artificial-intelligence-and-applied-machine-learning

[6-38] https://opennetworking.org/news-and-events/press-releases/onfs-sd-ran-now-fully-released-to-open-source/

[6-39] www.lfenergy.org/projects/

[6-40] https://github.com/microsoft/SynapseML

CHAPTER 7

Open Source Technology in Industry

Today there is hardly any industry that has not dabbled in open source software. Industries that have been around for more than a century, like automotive and agriculture, and the industries formed much more recently, like aerospace, have all embraced open source technologies. This chapter looks at how open source innovation is driving its usage in various industries and how industries influence the growth of new open source projects relevant to them.

Aerospace

The aerospace field has had only a few entrants in the past. These have mostly been big government-funded organizations such as the National Aeronautics and Space Administration (NASA) in the United States or the Indian Space Research Organization (ISRO) in India. However, there are new entrants in this field to capitalize on new areas such as space tourism and interplanetary travel. This has given a renewed push into the aerospace industry by non-government actors.

© Sachin Rathee and Amol Chobe 2022
S. Rathee and A. Chobe, *Getting Started with Open Source Technologies*,
https://doi.org/10.1007/978-1-4842-8127-7_7

Although it is a noble cause to allow humanity to technically explore options other than Earth in the event of a planet-threatening disaster, many government regulations still exist on how much of these technologies can be shared freely with anyone. This provides a severe roadblock in making aerospace technologies fully open source.

Few projects, however, have seen a path to being open sourced if they acquire proper clearances from the relevant organizations. NASA provides one such example. At NASA, one can submit a request to release their project as Open Source. Developers must send the proposal online to the Software Release Authority (SRA). This process assures that enough consideration is given to various aspects such as legal, export control, security, and compliance. Once approved, the project becomes available on NASA's GitHub page [7-1]. The projects are released under the NASA Open Source Agreement license (NOSA-1.3). The Open Source Initiative (OSI) has already approved this license. The list of these projects is expansive, but the following are some projects of interest.

- A real-time and virtual acoustic-environment rendering system to study spatial hearing in different environments such as virtual reality and video games

- Algorithms for text classification systems

- A 3D visualization system providing data analysis, scientific analysis, and situational awareness capabilities, which can be applied to robotics for research and exploration

- A simulation framework for creating an air traffic flow simulator at multiple levels of fidelity that allows simulations of the entire United States airspace to be finished in seconds (The pluggable nature of the framework enables higher-fidelity simulations to occur in some areas of the airspace concurrently with the low-fidelity simulation of the entire airspace.)

- A mission control framework for visualization of data for operation, analysis, and support of spacecraft missions

- Software for mission analysis, trajectory estimation, optimization, and predictions that aid in developing spacecraft trajectories, understanding orbit determination, and improving maneuvers, among other aspects of a mission, providing models of real-world parameters such as spacecraft and thrusters

Agriculture

The farming industry has been around for centuries. However, it has seen an evolution with changes in technology. Agriculture has gone through many broad iterations. Agriculture 1.0 is where it all started with a lot of manual effort from the farmers. It was essentially geographically adapted and followed traditional labor-intensive ways. Agriculture 2.0 included learnings from the green revolution, with farmers gaining access to better seeds, heavy machinery, pesticides, and fertilizers. Agriculture 3.0 is where hi-tech got introduced in farming, and it became more prevalent as we now move into Agriculture 4.0.

Agriculture 4.0 enables more cross-industry technologies and applications to develop smart agriculture. IoT (Internet of Things) plays an essential role in this. Several open source initiatives exist that have been used to build these devices. These include Raspberry Pi for open hardware with sensors like DHT22 for temperature and humidity. Many Eclipse Foundation projects [7-2], such as Eclipse Paho and Mosquitto, offer the protocols for connectivity. Several open source IoT platforms such as OpenRemote, ThingsBoard, and Thinger.io manage these devices in the field.

The following are other open source initiatives in this area.

- **Fiware**, developed by the Fiware Foundation [7-3], is a standard-based mechanism to build and integrate solutions for Smart Agrifood. It uses a wide range of technologies, including IoT sensors, wearables, GPS services, UAVs, robots, and drones operating in the field. Real-time data is then fed to systems helping to monitor the production line and support decisions to reduce waste and maximize outputs.

- **FarmOS** [7-4] is a web-based application for farm planning, record keeping, and management. A community of farmers, developers, researchers, and organizations has collaborated to provide a standard agricultural data collection and management platform.

The Linux Foundation has also started to divert attention to the agriculture sector and formed the AgStack Foundation [7-5] to provide growth mechanisms to several independent and relevant projects. AgStack's motivation is to create a shared community infrastructure for agricultural models, data sets, tools, and frameworks that fill a void in the current AgTech software ecosystem and provide easy and common access for content creators and consumers in the agriculture ecosystem. It aims to enable the following.

- Open and reusable software code for agronomically relevant models (crops, pests, weather, animals, etc.)

- Programmatic or API-based access to multiple sources of freely available public and proprietary data sets

- Online and mobile frameworks to build, contribute, use these data and accompanying models

AgStack Foundation aims not to create software applications but to focus on the software infrastructure needed to develop, manage, and run applications built by the users.

Automotive

Automotive industries have embraced technology to enable advanced features such as self-driving capability, immersive infotainment, and electric-powered vehicles, to name a few. With Linux as its core component, the Linux Foundation has embraced Automotive Grade Linux [7-6].

Automotive Grade Linux (AGL) is an open source project that brings together various members of the automotive value chain. These members include technology companies, automakers, and suppliers. AGL aims to collaborate and accelerate the development and use of a software stack for connected cars. The idea involves using Linux to develop an open platform from scratch. This platform can serve as the automotive industry standard for building new technologies that help the industry.

AGL consists of many expert groups that help define several relevant workstreams. The following are some prominent ones.

- The **AGL System Architecture Team** oversees the complete AGL technical architecture and manages the implementation of the AGL solutions.

- The **Container and Mesh Expert Group** is responsible for an in-vehicle container solution, orchestration component, and a service mesh that can be deployed as part of AGL.

- The **Reference Hardware System Architecture Expert Group** is responsible for defining the architecture of reference hardware.

- The **AGL Virtualization Expert Group** is responsible for designing and implementing virtualization solutions.

- The **Connectivity Expert Group** is responsible for the architecture and design of vehicle and cloud connectivity, firewalls, SmartDeviceLink, Remote Vehicle Interaction, connected cars, Bluetooth, Wi-Fi, and near-field communication (NFC).

Energy

The energy industry comprises fossil fuel industries, electrical and nuclear power industries, and the renewable energy industry. As the energy sector incorporates advances in technology, it faces numerous challenges concerning integrating new technology with existing legacy infrastructure. Current infrastructure needs to be improved to handle use cases such as transferring power based on supply and demand dynamics. Power transmission should be possible between individual producers (e.g., solar panels at homes producing excess energy and returning to the grid) and utility companies. To aggravate matters further, devices that form part of energy creation and consumption are not well integrated. It takes a lot of effort (e.g., programming) to get actionable information from these devices to understand their behavior.

The Linux Foundation founded LF Energy to enable faster innovation to handle challenges. LF Energy is an open source foundation involved with the power systems sector to deliver a standard functional architecture for the future power grid. It is working on several efforts [7-7] that include developing the following.

- Open source software components related to profile management and configuration of a power industry [7-8]

- Multiprotocol translation gateway for management of heterogeneous environments with disparate protocols over multiple systems in power systems [7-9]

- Software for support of microgrids that can enable the connection of homes, buildings, and other energy-consuming devices to energy-producing devices [7-10]

- Monitoring and control platforms for hardware systems being used [7-11]

- Toolkit for building standard methods of calculating normalized metered energy consumption. It provides methods for estimating energy efficiency savings at the meter [7-12]

- A smart grid standard and information exchange mechanism called Open Automated Demand Response (OpenADR) [7-13]

- An open source library to help with electrical grid simulation and modeling [7-14]

- Open source–based reference implementations and designs for running virtualized automation and protection applications for the power grid industry. This platform is intended to support a new generation of Digital Substations at grid nodes and edges [7-15]

- Smart Energy Framework for flexibility in offerings, ordering, forecasting, and settlement processes [7-16]

Gaming

The gaming industry is one of the entertainment segments revolutionized since the introduction of smartphones. Smartphones are now becoming the gaming consoles that you can carry with you anywhere, leading to heavy gaming penetration. The use of smartphones for gaming has also ushered in a new persona of game developers. These are individuals or small enterprises looking to cash in with the least investments overall for building games. To help keep the costs down, open source gaming tools come into play.

An essential tool called a *game engine* lies at the heart of game development. The game engine is a software development environment used to build games. It provides rendering for graphics and simulation of physical systems such as collisions, sound, networking, scripting, artificial intelligence, and animation.

Early video games were developed with gaming engines designed specifically for that game. These in-house developed gaming engines were primarily proprietary. Over time the engines started to be produced commercially. Third-party development of these gaming engines also opened doors for open source models.

Apart from the apparent reason for costs, open source gaming engines open the possibility of efficient adaptation of the needs of the games by making use of plugins needed for specific games. A game developer can use game engine plugins developed by another contributor rather than write it themselves. This saves time on game development tremendously.

Godot [7-17] is one of the best examples of open source platforms released under the MIT License. It offers a fully integrated game development environment for 2D and 3D game creation. It supports games creation in multiple programming languages such as C#, C++, and its own coding language called GDScript, which is similar to Python. Godot allows the deployment of games everywhere, whether it's mobile platforms like Android or iOS, desktop platforms like Linux, macOS, or Windows, or even consoles (e.g., Nintendo Switch, PlayStation 4, Xbox One). Games can also be exported to the web using web assembly and HTML. GitHub features plugins for Godot also that provide adaptation to specific needs [7-18].

Linux Foundation has also delved into 3D game and simulation technology by establishing an open 3D foundation (O3DF) [7-19]. One of the first projects under O3DF is Open 3D Engine (O3DE) [7-20]. O3DE is an Apache 2.0–licensed gaming engine that is multiplatform and supports 3D capabilities. The gaming engine enables developers and content creators to build 3D worlds and high-fidelity simulations for AAA games. Unlike its commercial counterparts, there are no fees or commercial obligations associated with using the O3DE engine.

Note   AAA or Triple-A games are video games produced or developed by a major publisher. These games have enormous budgets for development and marketing, rivaling some Hollywood movie budgets. On the other end of the spectrum are *indie* (short for *independent*) developers who publish games independently of any major publisher and with much smaller budgets.

Healthcare

The role of information technology in health care has seen many transformations in the past few years. Earlier open source technologies were used simply to bill and maintain records. However, now it is helping to modernize and increase the effectiveness of the entire health care system.

Growth in the use of information systems in healthcare has addressed many challenges. These include increased efficiency of back-office operations and reducing costs via automation. However, these information systems are disparate in many cases and make sharing any data highly complex. For example, sharing patient data with different healthcare providers—or even departments within a single healthcare provider—is a challenge that requires addressing with open solutions.

Health Level 7 International (HL7) [7-21] was formed to handle this interoperability. HL7 is an ANSI-accredited organization and provides a set of standards for the transfer, integration, sharing, and retrieval of electronic health information between applications used by various healthcare providers. The number 7 refers to the application layer of the Open System Interconnection model, as that's where these standards focus.

Note   OSI is a conceptual model that has standardized communication in a computing system.

Another software called OpenEMR [7-22] has provided lower-cost options for non-essential but otherwise higher expense management of electronic medical records (EMR). With this open source electronic health record system, small to medium-sized service providers can make EMR a reality with minimum investments compared to its proprietary counterparts.

OpenMRS (Open Medical Records System) was created to address the need for EMR in developing countries. The uniqueness of OpenMRS lies in the fact that the community maintains this platform as a base that implementers can use to create a customized EMR system according to the actual needs on the ground.

Open technologies can also play an essential role in fighting international-level pandemics such as COVID-19. The Linux Foundation formed the Linux Foundation for Public Health (LFPH) [7-23] to aid these efforts. Its mission is to use open source software to help public health authorities (PHAs) worldwide. The initial focus of LFPH has been to help PHAs deploy an app implementing the Google Apple Exposure Notification (GAEN) system.

Note   Google Apple Exposure [7-24] Notification is a protocol specification that helps to facilitate contact tracing. It was primarily built as a mechanism to contain the spread of the COVID-19 pandemic.

Manufacturing

Industry 4.0 is changing the way companies manufacture their products. Manufacturers incorporate new technologies such as artificial intelligence, machine learning, the IoT, and cloud computing in the production processes. These new technologies are converting existing factories into smart factories, bringing flexibility and resulting in better efficiencies through all phases of product manufacturing.

The Linux Foundation's Open Manufacturing Platform (OMP) [7-25] has led many efforts in this area since its formation in 2019. OMP is being developed with business and technology leadership from manufacturing companies (such as the BMW Group), technology solution providers (such as Red Hat), and systems integrators (such as CapGemini) to drive innovation across the manufacturing community. OMP effort involves multiple working groups addressing different technical areas.

- The **Manufacturing Reference Architecture Working Group** defines architectural artifacts such as blueprints on how different technological components fit together to provide a solution.

- The **IoT Connectivity Working Group** develops industrial-grade integration solutions for brownfield and greenfield industrial IoT equipment based on a cloud and edge approach to digitizing production lines. The following are current projects.

- OPC UA (Open Platform Communications United Architecture) Edge connector [7-26] converts OPC UA to a neutral format (e.g., MQTT or Kafka). It is built per OPC specifications (https://opcfoundation.org/developer-tools/specifications-unified-architecture)

- OPC UA test server [7-27] is implemented with Milo to test and verify different IoT connectivity scenarios in OMP

- **Semantic Data Structuring (SDS) Working Group** provides the ability to share, join and reuse heterogeneous data in manufacturing through comprehensive semantic data homogenization and contextual information. The number of devices that produce data and the number of applications that consume data is continuously growing in the manufacturing environment. The flow of data does not stop at the physical boundaries of a plant. The data is useful for IIoT software developers, mechanical engineers, and machine operators. This necessitates a standard mechanism to ease communication within this growing hardware, software, and people ecosystem. The SDS addresses this need. Their current projects include the following.

  - The BAMM Aspect Meta Model [7-28] allows the creation of models to describe the semantics of digital twins by defining their domain-specific aspects. The primary benefit of BAMM

136

is that it standardizes the creation of domain-specific models and makes them reusable. The created aspects can be used in several different digital twins.

Note   A *digital twin* is a virtual representation that serves as the real-time digital counterpart of a physical object or process.

- An SDS SDK (software development kit) [7-29] provides artifacts and resources to use, extend or integrate with the BAMM Aspect Meta Model.

- **Core services working group**: Robots, autonomous guided vehicles (AGVs), and cloud technology are essential in digitizing manufacturing plants. However, there is a significant effort to set this up and operate on the shop floor. This workgroup defines core services that help set up and monitor orders carried out by various autonomous robots.

Telecom

The telecommunication industry has been quite active in open source projects. Many open source projects that may not have started within the telecom domain have found their way into adoption by telecommunication companies as telecommunications architecture evolved. With the introduction of virtualization technologies, many open source components are now targeted for telecommunications networks. This means that open source models are now influencing the entire telecom architecture.

The ETSI organization has outlined the virtualization standard for telecommunications network architecture (see Figure 7-1). It defined various functional entities based on which the virtualization technology should be implemented. The standard allows independent development of these functions with interfaces to provide any necessary communication between themselves. This has led to multiple options within open source communities for many of these functions. ETSI does not provide implementation details of these interfaces and leaves it up to implementers of the functionality. However, this is still an important step as well-published APIs developed for these interfaces can allow developers to use them and build their products around them.

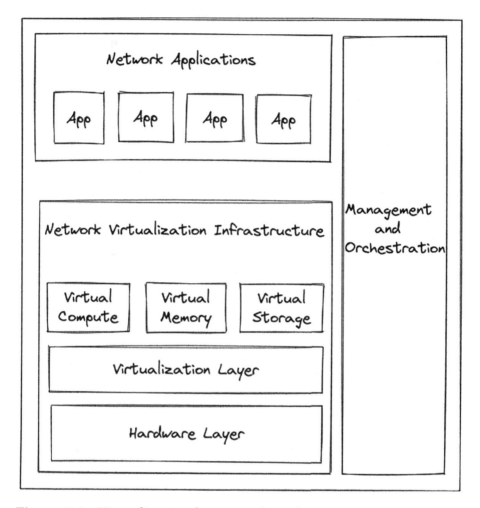

Figure 7-1. *Virtualization for network applications*

Telecommunications network applications, a.k.a. network functions, have traditionally been built by few network equipment providers. These functions have not been open sourced to a large extent. There are a few open source options, but they are usually used for specific testing purposes only, given the complicated requirements around their functionality.

Network function virtualization infrastructure is where most innovation has been concentrated in the open source communities. The disaggregation of apps and their underlying infrastructure with the help of virtualization allows the development of the applications and infrastructure separately. In the past, this was not the case; the network equipment vendors would provide a single piece of equipment with the infrastructure and applications together. This was done to achieve maximum performance benefits as the applications and infrastructure were tightly integrated. However, several additional open source projects now supplement the existing infrastructure projects to provide similar higher performance benefits.

The open source projects within the infrastructure domain were discussed in Chapter 6. These include KVM, OpenStack, Kubernetes, Ceph, OVN, and open hardware projects. All these projects apply here as well. However, let's look at additional projects that help drive better network performance for applications running on them.

Data Plane Development Kit (DPDK) [7-30] is an infrastructure project under Linux Foundation that helps process a network packet quickly. A network packet typically passes through the OS kernel into the user space, where the target application runs and consumes these packets. DPDK allows a faster path where the network packets can bypass the kernel and land directly into the user space.

Initially, Intel developed DPDK to run on x86-based CPUs. It now supports other CPU types, such as ARM. DPDK use is not limited to network applications developed for telecom only. It is also used by infrastructure components such as routers/switches to enable faster packet delivery between the applications. For example, the switching element of OVN (discussed in Chapter 6) called OVS (Open vSwitch) provides an implementation with DPDK, referred to as OVS-DPDK.

Another open source infrastructure project called FD.io [7-31] (Fast Data input/output) provides a collection of projects dealing with the creation of high-throughput, low-latency, and resource-efficient IO services suitable for multiple architectures (x86, ARM, and PowerPC) and deployment environments (bare metal, VM, container).

The key component within the project is the Vector Packet Processing (VPP), an open source framework providing routing and switching functionality. Along with VPP, FD.io leverages DPDK capabilities also in support of additional projects that help to accelerate the network data planes.

The management and orchestration (MANO) [7-32] functional block shown in Figure 7-1 manages the life cycle of network applications and services. It deploys the network applications and manages and monitors them during their operations.

The Open Network Automation Platform (ONAP) [7-33] is a MANO platform that delivers policy-driven orchestration and automation frameworks for virtual and physical network applications. It is hosted by Linux Foundation and is part of the Linux Foundation Networking (LFN) ecosystem. ONAP collaborates with several projects that are hosted within LFN today.

ETSI has a project called Open Source MANO (OSM) [7-34], which complements the work of ETSI and vice versa. ETSI-OSM capitalizes on the collaboration between the open source approaches and standardization benefits. This allows a more diverse set of developers and enterprises to contribute, leading to a more innovative product than what would usually be possible.

Cross-Industry Initiatives

The discussion in this chapter has been focused on open source solutions in individual industries until now. Many projects can span multiple industries, however. In fact, many projects begin in a particular industry but are adapted to other industries.

Edge

Edge computing is a computing paradigm where services are provided at or close to the physical location of either the user or data source. By positioning computing services closer to the users, the users benefit from faster and more reliable services leading to a better overall experience.

Edge computing is in use across multiple industries such as manufacturing, telecommunications, utilities, and transportation, to name a few. Many edge use cases are based on the need to quickly process data locally and meet service level requirements. Sending such data to centralized locations like public clouds for processing may not be an option.

To better understand this, let's look at a few examples. Sensors exist in factories to provide data on machines to ensure their smooth operations. They may exist in robots to gauge how well specific tasks are performed. They may also be in cars to provide better driving experiences. Data provided by these sensors need to be processed and acted upon quickly to take corrective actions before any mishaps occur.

In the entertainment industry, video game gamers expect faster response times and more immersive experiences, requiring real-time data processing. Video streaming services also benefit from more immediate delivery of high-resolution content with the help of content delivery networks (CDNs) at the edge. The telecommunication industry, which is set to deliver 5G, also requires thousands of sites closer to the user to deliver on the promise of faster speeds and higher data throughput.

To meet the demands of a myriad of industries that would benefit from the edge, Linux Foundation has formed LF Edge [7-35]. LF Edge hosts several projects which can be placed in one of the three stages.

Sandbox is the stage where projects that have future potential are introduced. Since LF Edge is part of the more established Linux Foundation, the projects get deeper alignment with other foundation projects through collaboration.

Incubation is where projects reach the next phase to provide more considerable impacts. Projects in this stage need to have a growth plan for getting to the next level.

Impact is the stage in which projects have reached their growth goals laid out in previous stages and are now on a self-sustaining cycle of support, maintenance, and development. These projects are typically used in production environments and have well-established project communities. They have contributors from at least two organizations. As of now, two projects have reached an impact stage and are worth discussing further in this book: Akraino [7-36] and EdgeX Foundry [7-37].

The Akraino project provides a set of application and infrastructure blueprints for the edge. It covers several use cases spanning artificial intelligence, 5G, and IoT. The Akraino community has created the blueprints focusing on the providers and enterprise edge domains.

EdgeX Foundry is an open source software framework that allows interoperability between heterogeneous applications and devices at the IoT Edge. EdgeX translates and transforms the information coming from devices and sensors and transports it to applications over network-based protocols in many formats and structures supporting new IoT data services and advanced edge computing applications, including AI and automation.

Blockchain

Blockchain technology, first popularized by the bitcoin cryptocurrency, has now been seen in broader use cases in multiple industries. At its core, blockchain is a distributed, decentralized, immutable digital ledger consisting of records called blocks. These blocks can record any transactions in various use cases. The use cases can include supply chain traceability in manufacturing, secure financial transactions in banking, better control of medical data in healthcare, and confirming product authenticity in retail, to name a few.

To help with the growth of the open source blockchain projects, Hyperledger Foundation [7-38], which is part of a larger Linux Foundation, brings together all the necessary resources and infrastructure to host several enterprise-grade blockchain software projects. Currently, it hosts many projects, such as Sawtooth [7-39], Fabric [7-40], Indy [7-41], and Iroha [7-42], that can be modeled into specific industry domain implementations. One such domain-specific project is Hyperledger Grid, which uses Sawtooth as back-end ledger technology. Hyperledger Grid [7-43] is a platform for building supply chain solutions. It provides tools that help with the acceleration of development for supply chain smart contracts and client interfaces.

Conclusion

As you can start to realize, open source has penetrated many industries today. In some industries (like telecommunications) where the penetration is relatively high, there is not only adoption of existing open source technologies, but new projects to better serve those industry needs are created regularly. In other industries with lesser use, you can still witness the use of open source with well-established software that has withstood the test of time, such as Linux-based operating systems.

Greater penetration is often restricted due to concerns around a need for competitive advantage. Note that the 80/20 principle can be applied to enterprises concerned with competition. Enterprises can use the work done in open source communities to meet 80 percent of their requirements. Any differentiated features that would form 20 percent of the requirements can be added via in-house development efforts or paid consulting.

Another reason for lesser adoption stems from the liability concerns at the forefront of enterprises considering open source software. Although many open source licenses are quite permissive to allow users to use as they wish (see Chapter 6), there can always be gray areas, as evident from the case involving Java APIs in the Oracle America Inc v. Google lawsuit [7-44]. The need for a good open source lawyer cannot be underestimated to handle these situations.

Scale and uniqueness of deployment have also been a concern for enterprises that believe that open source has never been tested for their specific environments. Although the deployment of open source software must undergo several iterations to get it right for a customer, this is true for any product deployed in a new environment. Even though the effort of testing the open source software lies with the enterprise using it, this can always be handled via contracting system integrators who are experts in a particular open source technology. This contract can be further extended to other areas, such as ongoing support where the enterprise would rather not get involved.

References

[7-1] https://github.com/nasa

[7-2] https://projects.eclipse.org

[7-3] www.fiware.org

[7-4] https://farmos.org

[7-5] https://agstack.org

[7-6] www.automotivelinux.org

[7-7] www.lfenergy.org/projects/

[7-8] www.lfenergy.org/projects/compas/

[7-9] www.lfenergy.org/projects/fledgepower/

[7-10] www.lfenergy.org/projects/hyphae/

[7-11] www.lfenergy.org/projects/gxf/

[7-12] www.lfenergy.org/projects/openeemeter/

[7-13] www.lfenergy.org/projects/openleadr/

[7-14] www.lfenergy.org/projects/powsybl/

[7-15] www.lfenergy.org/projects/SEAPATH/

[7-16] www.lfenergy.org/projects/shapeshifter/

[7-17] https://godotengine.org

[7-18] https://github.com/godotengine/awesome-
       godot#plugins-and-scripts

[7-19] https://o3d.foundation/

[7-20] www.o3de.org

[7-21] www.hl7.org

[7-22] www.open-emr.org

[7-23] www.lfph.io

[7-24] https://developer.apple.com/exposure-
       notification/

[7-25] https://open-manufacturing.org

[7-26] https://github.com/OpenManufacturing
       Platform/iotcon-opc-ua-connector-dotnet

[7-27] https://github.com/OpenManufacturing
       Platform/iotcon-opc-ua-server-milo

[7-28] https://github.com/OpenManufacturing
       Platform/sds-bamm-aspect-meta-model

[7-29] https://github.com/OpenManufacturing
       Platform/sds-sdk

[7-30] www.dpdk.org

[7-31] https://fd.io/

[7-32] www.etsi.org/deliver/etsi_gs/nfv-
man/001_099/001/01.01.01_60/gs_nfv-
man001v010101p.pdf

[7-33] www.onap.org

[7-34] www.etsi.org/technologies/open-
source-mano

[7-35] www.lfedge.org

[7-36] www.lfedge.org/projects/akraino/

[7-37] www.edgexfoundry.org

[7-38] www.hyperledger.org

[7-39] www.hyperledger.org/use/sawtooth

[7-40] www.hyperledger.org/use/fabric

[7-41] www.hyperledger.org/use/
hyperledger-indy

[7-42] www.hyperledger.org/use/iroha

[7-43] www.hyperledger.org/use/grid

[7-44] www.oyez.org/cases/2020/18-956

CHAPTER 8

Open Source Growth and Trends

This chapter focuses on the growth and trends of open source projects. The main objective of understanding this is to help you use open source for your benefit. The benefit can be in multiple forms, such as picking the correct repositories, licenses, and areas of involvement to become a major contributor and influencer in the open source world.

To understand the inner workings, you need to go deeper into open source project repositories. There are several repository hosting services available today. However, we selected a popular repository service with a large sample size for overall projects for our purpose. GitLab and GitHub are a few of the popular options. Based on GitLab's CEO, even though GitHub itself is closed source, it hosts most open source projects [8-1]. Although GitHub is a closed source project, it should not be a concern for our purposes, and we will explore it further.

Let's start by gauging the overall size of GitHub. When you look at GitHub search [8-2], you see that it hosts millions of repositories, and its growth in the past few years has been phenomenal. In general, the number of repositories on GitHub gives an idea of the extent of usage; however, this quantity must be of certain quality at the same time. To find the quality of projects, we used a stars metric. Per GitHub, starring a repository shows appreciation for the repository maintainer and their work. Many of GitHub's repository rankings depend on the number of stars a repository

S. Rathee and A. Chobe, *Getting Started with Open Source Technologies*, https://doi.org/10.1007/978-1-4842-8127-7_8

received [8-3]. If you use the number of stars as a quality parameter and run a query to visualize growth for repositories with at least one star, you see that the repositories have grown close to five times since 2014 (see Figure 8-1).

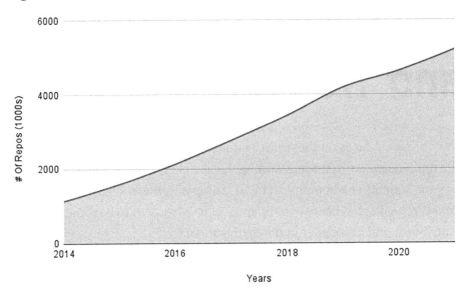

Figure 8-1. *GitHub repository growth*

Along with the repository, user growth is also an important parameter in understanding the viability and use of a platform. From the stats, you can see that there has been a similarly explosive growth in the number of users. When you compare 2014 to 2021, the numbers rose from 8 million to almost 80 million—a tenfold increase in seven years (see Figure 8-2). You can expect it to reach 100 million in a few years with that impressive growth.

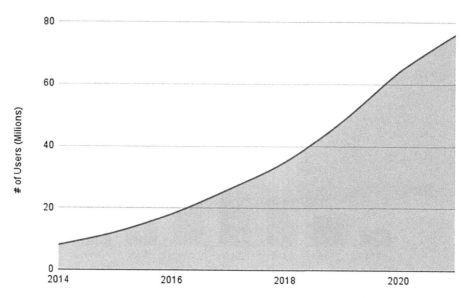

Figure 8-2. *GitHub user growth*

Given the repositories and user growth statistics, it would be prudent to look at open source projects on GitHub next. Let's apply a similar query but restrict it to only open source repositories in GitHub. We chose some of the most popular open source licenses: MIT, GPL, Apache, and LGPL.

The MIT License has risen from 76,000 repositories in 2014 to more than one million repositories at the start of 2021. MIT is the most widely used open source license on GitHub (see Figure 8-3).

151

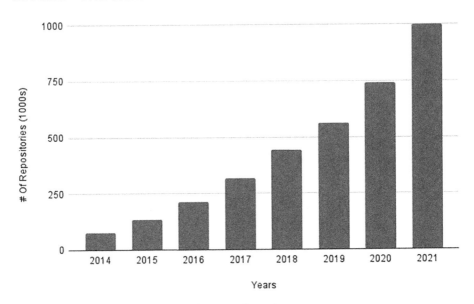

Figure 8-3. *Growth of MIT licensed projects*

The GNU General Public License comes in second place with almost 300,000 repositories as of 2021. It rose from nearly 30,000 in 2014, showing tenfold growth (see Figure 8-4).

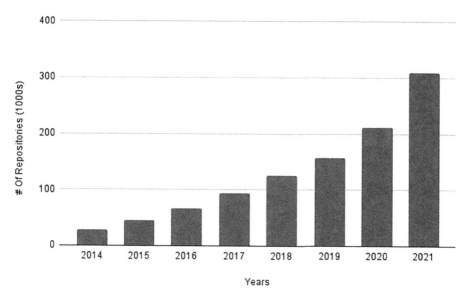

Figure 8-4. *Growth of GPL licensed projects*

Apache License 2.0 use has grown quickly, given the migration of all the Apache Foundation projects to GitHub in 2019 [8-4]. The growth has not slowed down post-migration either, and by 2021 the projects under Apache 2.0 increased further by 100,000 (see Figure 8-5). If these trends continue, Apache could climb to the second spot replacing GPL as the second most used open source license on GitHub.

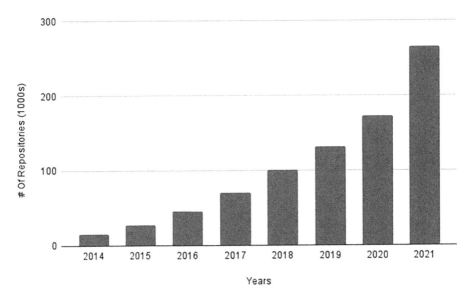

Figure 8-5. *Growth of Apache 2.0 License projects*

LGPL sits at the fourth spot, and its use has about a tenth of the Apache 2.0 when looking at 2021. The number of projects in 2021 sits at nearly 30,000 (see Figure 8-6). From this point on, all the other open source license use is relatively minor, and therefore, we are not going into those license specifics.

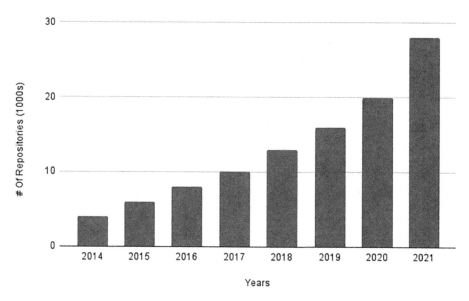

Figure 8-6. *Growth of LGPL licensed projects*

Popular Open Source Projects

Over the years, the repositories have been added and later archived; however, it would be meaningful to understand some of the open source projects that have become more popular than others. In this search, the popularity is assessed with the help of the number of stars these repositories have gained. We also eliminated any projects that have not been pushed in the last year to remove any dormant projects from the statistics (see Figure 8-7).

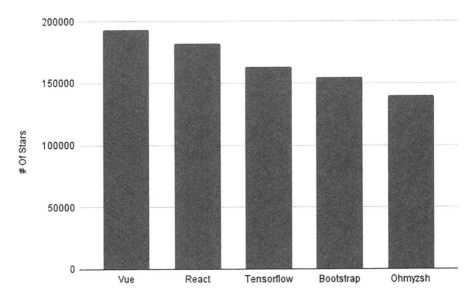

Figure 8-7. *The popularity of early open source projects*

Note   The push command uploads local repository content to a remote repository. In Git, pushing is how you transfer commits from your local repository to a remote repo. When applied to GitHub, a user first downloads a repository from GitHub on a local computer and makes code changes. Once changes are complete, the user pushes them back to GitHub [8-5].

GitHub contains several non-code repositories, which contain tutorials, books, and other artifacts. Some repositories are educational, such as algorithm implementations in specific languages or interview practice for developers. Once those repositories are eliminated, and you only compare ones with technology implementation, Vue stands out as the most popular repository, with close to 193,000 stars. This star count for Vue can be used to compare and gauge the popularity of other projects that you are familiar with.

Vue is the JavaScript framework. If you are familiar with other frameworks, such as AngularJS and ReactJS, you can easily understand how it fits in the world of JavaScript frameworks. Vue aims to create a more maintainable and testable codebase. It aims to be a progressive framework, which means it can be plugged into a part of the bigger application rather than requiring a complete redesign.

The second most popular on our list is the React project. React is the JavaScript framework for building user interfaces.

Important to note that the top two most popular projects are both based on JavaScript and use the MIT License.

The third on the list is the TensorFlow project. It provides an open source machine learning framework built using C++ and uses Apache License 2.0.

At number four, we are back into JavaScript and MIT License adoption with Bootstrap, an HTML, CSS, and JavaScript framework for developing responsive, mobile-first projects on the web. This gives you an idea of how web projects tend to be more popular for open source.

The next one on the list is an exciting entrant since it introduces shell programming to the top five projects. Oh My Zsh is an open source, community-driven framework for managing your Zsh configurations. Zsh is a shell designed for interactive use, although it is also a powerful scripting language. Many of the valuable features of Bash, Ksh, and Tcsh are incorporated into Zsh, making it a popular choice.

To provide some contrast, Linux stands at 126,000 stars. Although not far from number five, a few more repositories are between Oh My Zsh and Linux. Also, there are 33 repositories as of 2022 with more than 100,000 stars.

Web and mobile development technologies are the most popular types of open source projects. If you plan a project in that field, you will get a better following and recognition. Also, although AI and machine learning are currently hot topics, there is only one open source project in the 33 we searched. That may suggest an entry point to either get involved or build something new in that domain. The Oh My Zsh entry suggests that building a project on improving productivity for developers is very well received.

At this point, it makes sense to discuss other repositories that are non-code-based within the 33 we searched. Many of those are created to help the developer community. This is done by providing books, prewritten algorithms in a particular language, tutorials, interview preparation material, etc. These are great resources if you are just a beginner who wants to get better at specific technology, gain a new skill, or advance existing skills. These repositories have an immense following too.

Popular Users

GitHub is also home to millions of users. Some users are more influential than others. Let's measure the level of influence based on a metric called followers. Higher the number of followers for a particular user, the higher the popularity and influence. To understand who some of the top users on GitHub are, we ran a query to search for users with followers greater than 50,000 (see Figure 8-8).

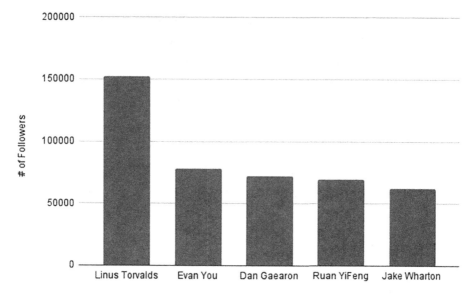

Figure 8-8. *Popularity of users*

Linus Torvalds, whose name is etched in history next to Linux, remains the most popular GitHub user. He currently has more than 150,000 followers. His followers are almost double the next popular user on GitHub. He has made at least 2,000 contributions each year in the last five years.

Evan You, who currently has about 78,000 followers, has been the most active member of the Vue project that he created in 2013. Evan has consistently made more than 2,000 contributions to the project, with up to 4,000 in just 2020.

Dan Gaearon, a Meta employee, is the third most followed user on GitHub. He currently has close to 72,000 followers. His work has been around project Redux, which he co-founded, and React. React has been discussed before, and Redux is the JavaScript library commonly used with frameworks like React or Angular to manage the application state.

User Ruan YiFeng sits at number four with around 69,500 followers. His activity has been focused on several training repositories. The most popular of those is the one that provides JavaScript, HTML, and CSS training.

Finally, user Jake Wharton, at number five, has 62,000 followers. Although known for many contributions in different areas, his most recent contributions have been under Cash app repositories.

The benefit of understanding these users is to study how the influencers work in the open source world. To be an influencer, you not only have to be involved in some of the crucial projects but be part of the founding circle. All the top users have made significant commits to projects but as you can see, merely making commits to the code is not enough; bringing a new technology to bear holds much more importance.

Language Statistics

When looking at the statistics for the popular languages on GitHub (see Figure 8-9), JavaScript leads the pack, followed by Python and Java. Back in 2008, when GitHub had just started, there was only a single repository, and it used the Ruby language.

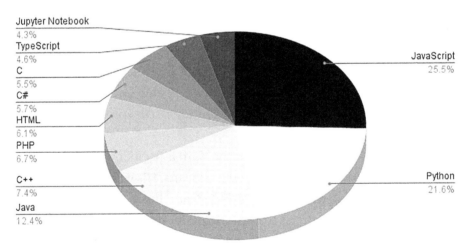

Figure 8-9. *Most popular languages*

JavaScript and Python have held their position well in open source projects. With the popularity of machine learning, Jupyter Notebook is now gaining popularity, especially after 2020. Figure 8-10 shows the top ten programming languages used over time.

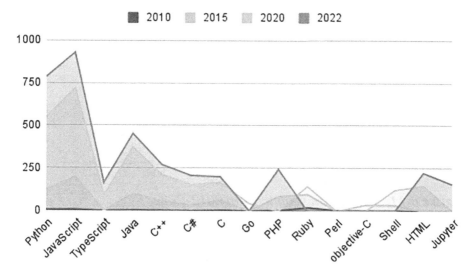

Figure 8-10. *Programming language use over time*

As the developer community evolves based on the requirements and use cases, it influences the programming languages used. One of the reasons JavaScript is very popular is that it can satisfy the requirements of beginners and advanced developers. It doesn't need any environment setup, and development can commence by using the developer's tools that come with the browser [8-6]. JavaScript can also run anywhere, including mobile devices, laptops, and tablets, on the server and client-side.

Angular, React, and Vue are the leading JavaScript libraries and frameworks. The most popular apps built using JavaScript are Candy Crush, Netflix, Facebook, and Uber. Figure 8-11 shows how JavaScript has remained popular over time.

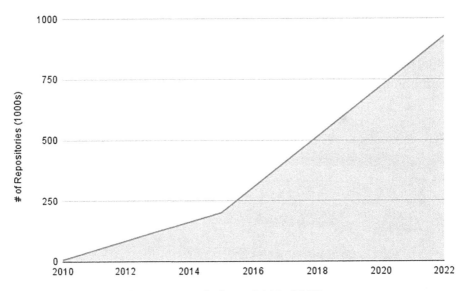

Figure 8-11. *JavaScript growth from 2012–2022*

The second most popular language is Python, known for its simplicity and flexibility. It is very easy to learn and widely adopted by the developer community. Google, Meta, and Amazon back Python.

A standard library is distributed with Python [8-7] that helps developers jumpstart the project quickly. Python package provides additional features used for complex application development.

Some of the most popular apps that use Python under the hood are Dropbox, Instagram, and Spotify. Due to the latest trends in cloud computing, machine learning, and big data, Python remains popular and continues its upward growth trend, as shown in Figure 8-12.

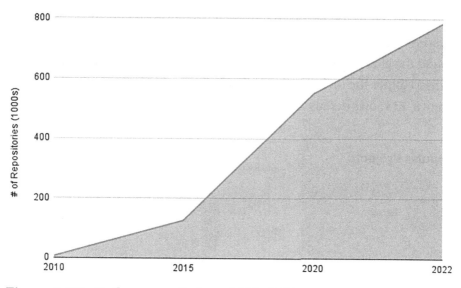

Figure 8-12. *Python growth from 2010–2022*

Emerging Domains in Open source

This section of the chapter focuses on emerging domains in open source like cryptocurrency, machine learning, and gaming. It also looks at the effects of COVID-19 in the open source world.

Cryptocurrency

Cryptocurrency is a medium of exchange that is digital, decentralized and encrypted. More than 4,000 users work on cryptocurrency projects spread over almost 50,000 repositories on GitHub. The most popular language used for cryptocurrency projects is JavaScript, followed by Python. Jupyter Notebook is a web-based interactive computing platform that is very popular in cryptocurrency projects.

The most popular project for cryptocurrency is Bitcoin, an experimental digital currency that enables instant payment anywhere around the globe. It is based on peer-to-peer technology. This project is licensed under the MIT License and has close to 62,000 stars on GitHub. Figure 8-13 shows details about the cryptocurrency projects.

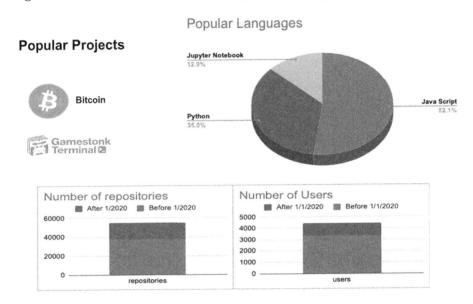

Figure 8-13. *Cryptocurrency projects*

The cryptocurrency domain is growing, and so is the interest in the open source community about it. There are more than 5,000 different cryptocurrencies in the market, and most of the development for cryptocurrency is done using open source technologies.

Machine Learning

Jupyter Notebook remained the most popular platform in the community for developing machine learning projects. There are more than 500,000 repositories on machine learning on GitHub, supported by close to 80,000 users (see Figure 8-14).

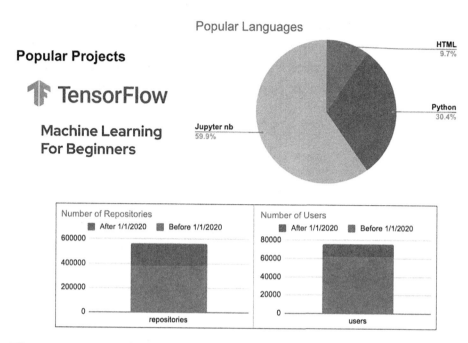

Figure 8-14. *Machine learning projects*

TensorFlow is the most popular project on GitHub for machine learning, with more than 3,000 contributors. This project has 163,000 stars. The second most popular project, with 29,000 stars, is the Microsoft-led and developed Machine Learning for Beginners curriculum. This project is under the MIT License.

Gaming

A gaming engine is a software development framework that simplifies and speeds up the development process for games. As per the trend on GitHub, JavaScript remains popular in the gaming world because of its ability to target multiple platforms.

Gaming has more than one million repositories, and more than 12,000 users contribute to them (see Figure 8-15). Godot, a game engine to create 2D and 3D games from a unified interface, is the most popular project, with close to 1,600 contributors and 46,300 stars. Godot is released under the MIT License.

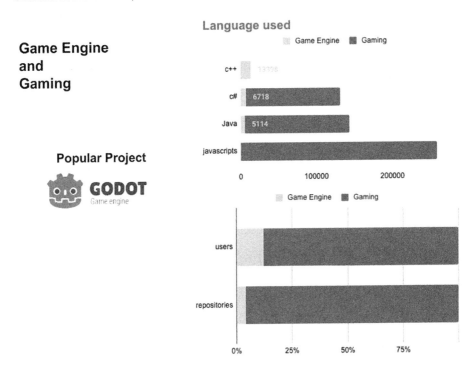

Figure 8-15. *Gaming projects*

COVID-19

The COVID-19 pandemic is an ongoing global pandemic of coronavirus disease, which started in 2019. This pandemic is a great example of how open source propels innovation in times of great need. There were close to 196,000 repositories created in two years, concentrating on analyzing and finding the patterns and trends that help fight this global pandemic. More than 3,000 users are contributing to these projects.

The most popular project on GitHub is COVID-19 Data Repository by the Center for Systems Science and Engineering (CSSE) at Johns Hopkins University [8-8]. This project is a data repository for a COVID-19 visual dashboard operated by CSSE. This project has 28,300 stars. JavaScript remains popular with the community as a programming language for COVID-19-related projects.

Commercial Organization's Active Contribution

The Open Source Contributor Index (OSCI) [8-9], an open source project, tracks and measures open source activity on GitHub by commercial organizations. According to December 2021 data, Microsoft, Google, and Red Hat have the most active contributors to open source projects (see Figure 8-16).

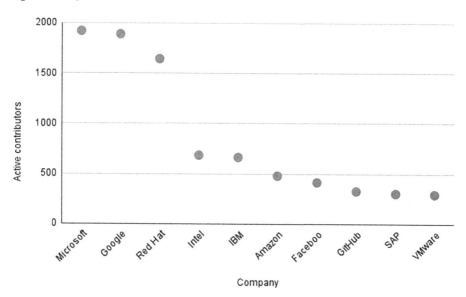

Figure 8-16. *Active contributors from companies*

Note the trend between the top three companies—Microsoft, Google, and Red Hat—from 2016 to 2020, as shown in Figure 8-17. Each of these companies' active contributors has increased over the years. This shows that organizations are encouraging employees to participate in open source communities. You can expect this trend to grow over the years as new technologies keep getting introduced in open source communities.

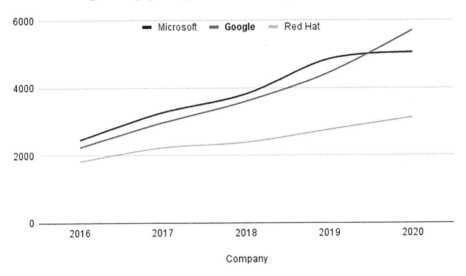

Figure 8-17. *Active contribution growth*

Conclusion

This chapter discussed the current growth trends of open source projects and many popular languages based on GitHub activity. As new projects in cryptocurrency, machine learning, and gaming developed, open source adopted the latest technologies and tools suitable for those domains to drive innovation faster. For example, in machine learning, the Jupyter Notebook, a relatively new technology, is embraced by the community to develop new ML projects. Its adoption continues to grow with every new machine learning project added.

A MarketsandMarkets report [8-10] projects that the open source services market, which was $21.7 billion in 2021, is expected to grow more than $50 billion by 2026—a whopping growth rate of 130 percent. This trend leads us to believe that industry adoption of open source software will continue to climb in the upcoming years.

References

[8-1] https://about.gitlab.com/blog/2016/07/20/gitlab-is-open-core-github-is-closed-source/

[8-2] https://github.com/search/

[8-3] https://docs.github.com/en/get-started/exploring-projects-on-github/saving-repositories-with-stars

[8-4] https://github.blog/2019-04-29-apache-joins-github-community/

[8-5] www.atlassian.com/git/tutorials/syncing/git-push

[8-6] https://developer.chrome.com/docs/devtools/

[8-7] https://docs.python.org/3/library/

[8-8] https://github.com/CSSEGISandData/COVID-19

[8-9] https://github.com/epam/OSCI

[8-10] https://venturebeat.com/2021/09/21/open-source-services-market-on-course-to-become-50b-industry/

CHAPTER 9

The Path Forward

Throughout this book, you explored many aspects of open source technology. However, to build a better and sustainable path for it, the following aspects should be examined.

- How can open source technologies be introduced in school curriculums?

- How should new entrants to the world of open source select projects for contribution?

- How can we ensure the continuous adoption of open source by enterprises in the future?

- What role does open source play in the latest technological innovations?

Due to the COVID-19 pandemic, the world of technology has changed substantially. Remote work environments have become the new norm for companies, bringing in the changes associated with it. Since most industries have gone remote, privacy, security, and migration to the cloud have become the most important topics. Due to talent gaps, many companies are not yet well equipped for these changes. Hiring new talent and training existing staff has become the top priority.

The Linux Foundation published its *2021 Open Source Jobs Report* in September 2021 [9-1]. This report sheds light on the need for open source talent in the industries and how hiring managers prioritize hiring open source talent.

© Sachin Rathee and Amol Chobe 2022
S. Rathee and A. Chobe, *Getting Started with Open Source Technologies*,
https://doi.org/10.1007/978-1-4842-8127-7_9

Figure 9-1 shows why developers chose a career in open source technology. One of the top reasons is that open source builds cutting-edge technologies adopted in the industry already. This allows developer skills to be marketable immediately to many enterprises. This survey also shows that professionals are genuinely passionate about using open source and value the collaborative approach of the open source development model.

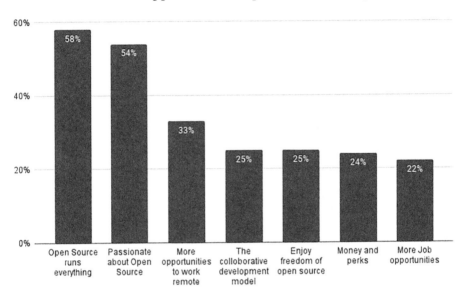

Figure 9-1. *Why professionals choose open source*

This report also claims that 50 percent of hiring managers were planning to increase their hiring of open source expertise compared to the previous six months. Ninety-seven percent of hiring managers emphasized hiring open talent as the highest priority.

Figure 9-2 shows the technologies that hiring managers are prioritizing. Due to the pandemic, cloud adoption has seen significant growth. The cloud offers capabilities to centralize infrastructure management, thus helping with remote accessibility, observability, and remediation. Kubernetes, a container orchestrator that manages cloud-native applications, has seen an increase in contributors by 88 percent

172

in the last three years. Demand for cloud and container skills sits at the number-one spot. After the cloud, other infrastructure technologies, such as Linux and networking, are also in significant demand sitting in the second and third positions, respectively.

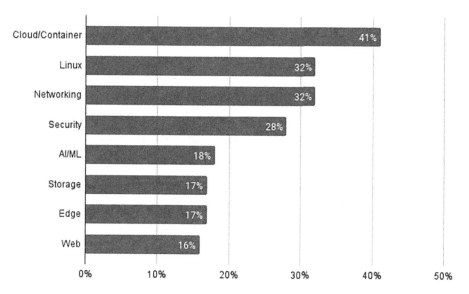

Figure 9-2. *Skills prioritized by hiring managers*

To support the growth and development of such skills, there is a strong need for enablement by providing easy access to training and certifications programs to the workforce. To make sure that these demands are met early, we need to focus on open source education during the early years of school and college.

Open Source in Education

Open source provides opportunities for students as well as teachers to benefit. Students can learn open source technologies with the help of an updated curriculum and prepare for the competitive markets. Teachers

173

can teach open source technologies by adopting open source for building content and educational tooling. Schools and universities are helping by including open source in curricula and building open source software for educational purposes. Many companies are also creating programs to help further open source education.

Curriculum

Few schools and colleges are already adopting open source methods, principles, and projects. However, we have still not seen open source become a mainstream subject in the curriculum coursework; only a handful of the universities/colleges offer open source courses.

- The Rochester Institute of Technology (RIT) noticed the need for open source talent in industries. It launched the first minor degree program in Free and Open Source Software and Free Culture [9-2].

- Michigan Technological University (MTU) has a website dedicated to open source projects and has dedicated groups who work and collaborate on different open source projects. MTU also offers open source–specific courses, and the most popular one is an open source 3D printing course [9-3].

Due to the high demand for open source talent, it's a massive opportunity for the other institutes to follow the footsteps of the RIT and MTU and offer courses to create the next generation of the open source talent pool. Today, most students rely on resources like the Linux Foundation, Coursera, and Udemy for basic open source education.

Some educators are doing their part by taking initiatives to teach PK-12 students about open source technologies like Linux operating systems and Raspbian OS [9-4]. This is usually done via various afterschool clubs [9-5].

Software Tools

Colleges and universities are using open source software tooling to build learning and research platforms as this helps them reduce the cost and allow flexibility.

- Universities like Indiana University, the University of Southern Queensland, and Brandeis University are part of the Open Source Initiative (OSI) and collaborate to develop open source software for education [9-6].

- The Open Science Framework (OSF) is a free scholarly web tool that focuses on transparency, sharing, collaboration, and visibility of research outputs at the institutional level. Many premier education institutes like Brown University, Carnegie Mellon University, Boston University, and many more are members of this project [9-7].

- In Europe, Erasmus Without Paper, a key initiative of the European Education Area, aims to bring the Erasmus administration into the twenty-first century by going digital [9-8]. They have created an initiative called Open Source University Alliance to help higher education institutions meet the latest digital transformation demand. The alliance creates an open source code repository and educational tools for the higher education community [9-9].

- Universities like Louisiana State University, La Trobe University, the University of Zagreb, and many others converge on learning management systems. These platforms help with the creation of courses, assessment of students, and sharing of materials. Moodle is a popular open source platform used extensively for these purposes [9-10].

Industry Programs

Industries are also doing their bit to encourage students and aspiring professionals to participate in open source programs. The following describes some examples.

- DigitalOcean's annual Hacktoberfest program [9-11] encourages aspiring developers to submit four or more pull requests to projects and gives developers swag as a token of appreciation. The main idea is to encourage an individual to start with open source.

- Major Hacking League (MHL) [9-12] provides a 12-week internship where students collaborate on open source projects.

- Season of KDE [9-13] is an outreach program that encourages students to participate in projects that benefit the KDE ecosystem. KDE is a software community that develops free and open source software.

- Google's Season of Docs [9-14] program equips technical writers to improve their documentation for open source projects. It helps them gain experience and raises awareness of open source.

- Google Summer of Code (GSoC) [9-15] focuses on bringing new contributors into open source software development.

- The Linux Foundation's Linux Kernel Mentorship program [9-16] is a 12-week program for aspiring Linux kernel developers to contribute and work toward making the kernel more secure and sustainable.

Initiating Open Source Projects

Initiating open source software is an enormous task that requires understanding all the domains of software development and working with communities. Fortunately, open source communities have honed their learning and put them into best practices. These best practices have led to collaboration and transparency within the communities, and they should be applied whenever starting an open source project. These practices include the following.

- Focus on the business need for the project. Understand what the project should serve and if its requirements and the business needs are critical enough to initiate an open source project.

- Before starting the project, investigate if similar projects already exist. If there are similar projects, investigate how they can be used rather than initiating a new project.

- Pick the open source project license that fits your delivery model.

- Decide on the name and branding for the project such that it identifies the project uniquely.

- Decide on the programming language and tools to use for the project. The correct language and tooling should be based on relevance and popularity. Relevance guarantees that it's a good fit for a project from a performance and manageability point of view. Popularity ensures the availability of enough talent.

- Start with a README file for the project, which goes over the details, such as the following.

- Key objectives

- Relevance

- Information on how to get started

- Roadmap and timelines

- Provide detailed contributors/participations guidelines [9-17] that cover the following.

  - Environment setup details

  - Information on bug reporting

  - Maintains responsibility matrix listing key members

  - New feature request procedures

- Establish a project code of conduct to set up ground rules for participants. This helps create a welcoming environment for all the contributors.

- Regularly check the quality of the project based on bug filing and resolution reports.

- Evaluate the project periodically to make sure it is delivered as per the timeline.

- Periodically check the number of contributors in the community and their level of influence to ensure that the community is strong.

- Market your projects on social media sites like LinkedIn, Twitter, and different interest forums to create ample awareness of the project.

Getting Involved in Open Source with Enterprises

For open source culture to succeed, enterprises must continue to support it. Enterprise support, in turn, can be gained by providing enough talent to support their open source endeavors. For individuals who want to get into open source for a career and support this mission, there are a few accomplishments that companies look for in a candidate. These accomplishments are generally in the following key areas.

- The quality and quantity of an individual's contributions to an open source project and its acceptance within the project

- Influence in the open source project community could translate to positions candidates hold on relevant project steering committees

- An individual's public presence is gauged by the quality and quantity of workshops, presentations, or blogs delivered by the candidate that advocates the project

---

Note   Contributing to open source is not limited to being a developer. You can contribute in different ways by writing documentation, opening the bug issues, suggesting improvements, or creating new features proposals.

The candidate should perform due diligence on the employer too. Before joining a company, find out details on the company's open source projects adoption and contributions. Start by focusing on the following key areas.

- Check the company's open source projects contributions. Large contributions ensure a company's commitment to open source.

- Check if they are leading any open source project. Having employees in positions such as team lead creates a leadership position for the company in the industry.

- Check the company's open source project goals and roadmaps because this helps you understand the company's vision.

- Check that company has put in enough resources to market its open source projects on social media channels. This ensures that open source projects are given enough priority in the company.

- Check the programming language and tools used and their relevance to today's technology standards. Working on popular languages ensures future career growth opportunities.

Upcoming Innovations

Looking at the technology maturing in the next one or two years, we noticed that Metaverse and Web 3.0 are gaining a lot of attention lately [9-18]. Web 3.0 mainly focuses on Internet control, whereas the metaverse concentrates on how users will experience the Internet in the future.

Web 3.0

Web 3.0 is the third generation of the Internet that uses decentralized ways to interconnect data to deliver a quicker and more personalized user experience. One of the main pillars of Web 3.0 is *open* (i.e., built using open source software by an open and accessible community and executed in full view of the world). One of the most popular open source projects is Polkadot, which the Web3 Foundation founded. The foundation aims to facilitate a user-friendly decentralized Internet [9-19]. There are already more than a thousand repositories on GitHub focusing on Web3.0 domain development.

Metaverse

The metaverse is a simulated digital environment that uses concepts from social media along with virtual reality (VR), augmented reality (AR), and blockchain to create digital spaces. These digital spaces emulate the real world and provide rich user interaction.

Open source will be a key target for developers when it comes to metaverse as content and user adoption are the main backbone. An *open simulator* is one of the popular open source projects in this domain. It is a multiplatform, multiuser 3D application server that can be used to create a virtual environment [9-20].

According to Gartner Inc., in the next five to ten years, certain technologies will be disrupting the industry [9-21]. Next, let's look at them and discuss how open source software can help.

Multiexperience

The user *multiexperience* is the next step in digital transformation. A multiexperience concentrates on multichannel user experiences. It uses a single application across various digital touchpoints and uses a combination of interaction modalities like voice, vision, motion, and touch to interact with other users. One great example of a multiexperience is the Domino's AnyWare online ordering platform that allows customers to order pizza using different modes of communication, including Alexa, Google Home, Slack, smart TVs, the web, and mobile apps, among others. Gartner predicts that by 2026, 75 percent of the enterprises will use a multiexperience platform to build digital apps (mobile, conversational, and progressive web) [9-22]. Convertigo is a low code/no code development platform for building multiexperience applications [9-23].

Note   Low-code development platforms help deliver applications faster than the traditional method by abstracting and automating many steps.

Quantum Computing

Quantum computing is a new paradigm in the computation world that uses quantum physics to perform calculations. Quantum computing is approaching the mainstream, and organizations like the Open Source Foundation (QOSF) are helping with that. QOSF is committed to improving the standardization and quality of open source software in quantum computing [9-24]. Companies believe that open source technologies will help them adopt quantum computing faster [9-25].One example is Qiskit SDK, a project by IBM focused on developing quantum computing [9-26].

Decentralized Finance

Decentralized finance, or DeFi, is a digital financial infrastructure built on blockchain technology that theoretically puts an end to reliance on brokerages, central authorities, or government agencies to approve financial transactions. Gartner predicts that by 2024, 20 percent of large enterprises will use digital currencies [9-27]. The DeFi protocols and applications are all open to inspection and forking by anyone. One popular open source project is Rainbow, an Ethereum (a cryptocurrency) wallet [9-28]. A curated list of DeFi open source projects is on GitHub [9-29].

NFT (Non-Fungible Token)

Non-fungible tokens allow anyone to sell and buy unique digital items and keep track of ownership using blockchain technology. Although NFTs sales rose to $2.47 billion in the first half of 2021 [9-30], this is still the tip of the iceberg. Gartner Inc. predicts NFTs are five years away from mainstream adoption [9-31].

Dept, a digital agency, launched an open source platform called AlgoMart, which helps brands launch their own NFTs [9-32].

Named Data Networking

Named Data Networking is an NSF research project. This project was started in 2010 to create the architecture for the future Internet. Named Data Networking (NDN) changes the network communication model from delivering packets to destinations identified by IP addresses to fetching data packets by names. Gartner expects NDN will be adopted in the mainstream by 2030 [9-33]. There are many open source projects initiated by NDN that are in the early stages [9-34].

Conclusion

Open source software is at the heart of all technologies used in our daily lives. It supports innovation in cloud computing, handheld devices, and even the ubiquitous Internet. Even with the prevalence of open source software, we may be only scratching the surface.

Open source has democratized innovation substantially. Today, anyone can start innovating and developing software collaboratively and efficiently. Businesses are harvesting this innovation substantially. To continue its current upward trend, open source projects must rely on sustainable and successful businesses that have a stake in the open source model. Continuous acceptance by businesses guarantees future support of the open source movement.

Although businesses and individuals benefit from the open source model, open source projects benefit society. A better world is built with inclusive and open technologies.

References

[9-1] http://teachingopensource.org/linux-foundation-2021-open-source-jobs-report/

[9-2] www.rit.edu/study/free-and-open-source-software-and-free-culture-minor

[9-3] https://opensource.mtu.edu/about.html

[9-4] https://opensource.com/article/17/12/linux-and-raspberry-pi-education

[9-5] https://opensource.com/article/18/3/linux-forward-schools

[9-6] https://opensource.org/node/798

[9-7] www.cos.io/products/osf-institutions

[9-8] https://ec.europa.eu/education/education-
       in-the-eu/european-education-area_en

[9-9] http://ecahe.eu/open-source-university-
       alliance/

[9-10] https://moodle.org

[9-11] https://hacktoberfest.digitalocean.com

[9-12] https://fellowship.mlh.io

[9-13] https://season.kde.org

[9-14] https://developers.google.com/
        season-of-docs

[9-15] https://summerofcode.withgoogle.com

[9-16] https://wiki.linuxfoundation.org/lkmp

[9-17] https://docs.github.com/en/communities/
        setting-up-your-project-for-healthy-
        contributions/setting-guidelines-for-
        repository-contributors

[9-18] https://blocking.net/13194/gartner-vice-
        president-web-3-0-will-replace-web-2-0-
        in-5-7-years/

[9-19] https://polkadot.network

[9-20] http://opensimulator.org/wiki/Main_Page

[9-21] www.gartner.com/en/newsroom/press-
        releases/2021-08-23-gartner-identifies-
        key-emerging-technologies-spurring-
        innovation-through-trust-growth-and-change

[9-22] www.gartner.com/doc/reprints?id=1-26YPI
        7NO&ct=210728&st=sb

[9-23] www.convertigo.com

[9-24] https://qosf.org

[9-25] https://research.ibm.com/blog/quantum-
development-roadmap

[9-26] https://qiskit.org

[9-27] www.gartner.com/en/newsroom/press-
releases/2021-12-16-gartner-says-20-
percent-of-large-enterprises-will-use-
digital-currencies-by-2024

[9-28] https://github.com/rainbow-me/rainbow

[9-29] https://github.com/ong/awesome-
decentralized-finance

[9-30] www.coindesk.com/markets/2021/07/06/
nft-sales-climb-to-247b-in-first-
half-2021-report/

[9-31] https://protos.com/gartners-hype-cycle-
nfts-could-be-5-years-from-mainstream-
acceptance/

[9-32] www.deptagency.com/en-us/insight/
dept-launches-first-ever-open-
source-platform-for-creating-an-nft-
marketplace/

[9-33] www.gartner.com/en/newsroom/
press-releases/2021-08-23-gartner-
identifies-key-emerging-technologies-
spurring-innovation-through-trust-
growth-and-change

[9-34] https://github.com/named-data

Index

A

Accredited Standards Committee X9 (ASC X9), 32
Active contributors, 167, 168
Advanced Micro Devices (AMD), 85
Aerospace, 125, 126
AGL System Architecture Team, 129
AGL Virtualization Expert Group, 130
Agriculture, 125, 127, 128
AgStack Foundation, 128, 129
AgTech software ecosystem, 128
Akraino project, 143
Alpha-Omega Project, 70
Analytics Zoo, 109
Android-based devices, 23
Android Open Source Project (AOSP), 42
Apache License, 41–43, 88, 92, 94, 153, 157
Apache License 2.0, 42, 88, 92, 94, 153, 157
Apache Software Foundation (ASF), 41

Apache 2.0, 42, 51, 133, 153, 154
Application-specific integrated circuit (ASIC), 113
Architectural artifacts, 135
Artificial intelligence (AI), 99
    data preparation, 103
    deployment, 106
    framework/tooling, 106, 107
    Keras, 107
    ML workflow, 104
    Neo project, 107
    PyTorch, 108
    simulation, 104
    TensorFlow, 107
    Theano, 108
    training, 104
    transformation, 103
Augmented reality (AR), 181
Authentication systems, 68
Automotive Grade Linux (AGL), 31, 119, 129
Automotive industry, 28, 129
    AUTOSAR, 29, 30
    CCC, 30, 31
    5GAA, 28, 29
    open source, 31, 33

Printed in the United States
by Baker & Taylor Publisher Services